FS Books:
Sport Fish of Florida
Sport Fish of the Gulf of Mexico
Sport Fish of the Atlantic
Sport Fish of Fresh Water
Sport Fish of the Pacific

Baits, Rigs & Tackle
Sportsman's Best: Snapper & Grouper
Annual Fishing Planner
From Hook to Table

Florida Sportsman Magazine
Shallow Water Angler Magazine
Florida Sportsman Fishing Charts
Lawsticks
Law Boatstickers

Edited by Joe Richard and Florida Sportsman Staff
Art Direction by DKW Designs, Drew Wickstrom
Illustrations by Joe Suroviec and Ron Romano
Copy Edited by Jerry McBride and Amy Richard

First Edition
First Printing
Copyright 2004 by Florida Sportsman
All Rights Reserved
Printed in the United States of America
ISBN 0-936240-31-8

www.floridasportsman.com

SNAPPER
&GROUPER

CONTENTS

SB

SPORTSMAN'S BEST
SNAPPER & GROUPER

14

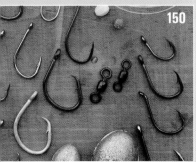

118

150

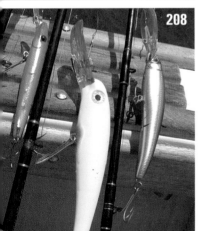

Meet the Writers

T his is the first book in the "Sportsman's Best" series, published by *Florida Sportsman* magazine. Four captains from different corners of Florida were utilized to write parts of the book, adding their many years of knowledge. Each has spent approximately 30 years on the water, for a total of 120 years of fishing experience, and they've dispensed their knowledge here.

The DVD in the back of this book has more than an hour of educational footage. Three captains give their best snapper and grouper tips.

This is a must-read for anyone heading out in coastal waters, who can learn something about the many species of snapper or grouper found in U.S. waters, or The Bahamas and Caribbean.

SNAPPER & GROUPER

JOE RICHARD Snapper & Grouper Editor

Joe Richard is an editor with Florida Sportsman, and served eight years as editor of Tide magazine. He's fished offshore in the Gulf of Mexico since 1968, guided offshore in Texas, and in both Steinhatchee and Fernandina in Florida.

"Those fish-sore hands are proof you've been offshore."

RICK RYALS

Rick Ryals is a ball of energy. He is director of the Florida Sportsman radio network, sells advertising and writes for the magazine, and has fished offshore of Mayport and St. Augustine for 30 years.

"I hadn't slept in days, anticipating our big adventure."

GARY FOLDEN

Gary Folden is also part of the Florida Sportsman radio network, covering fishing in the Tampa-St. Petersburg area. He's been guiding out of Clearwater Beach for 30 years.

"I always keep a lookout for my next honeyhole."

GEORGE MITCHELL

George Mitchell has lived his entire life in South Florida, and also co-hosts a radio show for Florida Sportsman. He fishes the coral reefs north of Miami down into the Keys, running a charterboat just north of Key Largo.

"It keeps me coming back to fish the reef country."

Bottom fishing gets in the blood. For many, no sport is better in the outdoor world.

JOE RICHARD

The history of snapper/grouper fishing in the Southeast isn't quite as romanticized an occupation as the New England bottom fishery, which has spawned famous novels and movies, such as *Captains Courageous*, written by world author Rudyard Kipling.

Red snapper (and soon after) grouper were found in 1840, when that virgin fishery was amazingly discovered right off Pensacola beach. That's the year fishermen began to realize there was some serious action to be found offshore in the Gulf of Mexico. Bottom fishing from Florida up to North Carolina would follow in later years.

Bottom fishing gets in the blood and for many fishermen, there is nothing better in the outdoor world. Only a few years ago the sport was dominated by slow partyboats, gruff fishermen wearing old clothes, sturdy tackle, smelly bait and a great many fish dragged over the rail, large and small. Private boats were few and finding fish was tough. That's all changed over the years with many refinements.

Joe Richard beside his rental kayak in the Florida Keys. First mate Amy Richard uses light tackle on a Belize reef.

How about owning your own, high-tech boat with a livewell, and finding new spots offshore where grouper and snapper hit with complete abandon? And returning with accurate navigation, and having the satisfaction of watching your friends quickly get "bowed-up" on big fish. That's a Southern expression meaning the rod is bowed, or deeply bent. It's a good sign that snapper or grouper are home and hungry.

With bottom fishing, you stay busy. There's no time to read an entire book, like many have while trolling all day. You drop the bait deep, and prepare yourself for upwards of 50 kinds of fish that might be lurking below. One can often hook two or three fish on a multi-hook bottom rig, with each one a different species. Or drop a single hook down, to get slammed by a 50-pound grouper. All of this makes for some difficult Monday mornings for

many of us, after plowing through waves all weekend and wrestling fish up from the bottom.

After being away from bottom fishing for too long, just the smell of bait and salt on the hands after a long day on the water can be oddly pleasing. Those fish-sore hands are reward and proof that you've been offshore again. And now, if the wind will just lay down by next weekend...

RICK RYALS

Snapper and grouper fishing got into my blood real early. My fondest memory happened more than 30 years ago, when we ventured 45 miles off Jacksonville on an overnight trip in a 23-foot boat. For years we'd watched these long-range commercial snapper boats unload huge catches of oversized red snapper, and this was our chance to join in the bonanza.

We knew we needed two days of perfect weather. That would give us a chance to run four hours offshore, giving us enough time to hunt for good bottom before sunset. We'd spend the night, fish the next morning, and head home early enough to make it back before dark. With only a compass, we'd never

There is satisfaction in seeing your friends "bowed up" on big, strong bottom fish.

A sunrise bite ahead of the weekend crowd may produce instant action and quick results. Rick Ryals and Denny Young seem happy with this catch.

navigate straight back, but with enough daylight and familiar beach landmarks, we'd make it just fine.

Finally arriving far offshore, we started marking good bottom and it was time to drop baits. Trouble was, after this long voyage, all we could find were triggerfish and red porgy. We spent the rest of that day unhooking those two kinds of fish. There must have been miles of them. Every bait was instantly consumed. With sunset upon us, we picked out a big underwater ledge and threw out the anchor. The boat settled right over it. Dropped some baits down. You guessed it, more triggers and porgies.

Night fell. I hadn't slept in days, anticipating our big adventure. The unforgettable sight of millions of stars overhead had just about put me under. But it was time for the day's last drop to the bottom. As soon as the bait hit, my rod doubled over. The other guys were groaning too, hooked up to big fish. The triggerfish that had tormented us all day had gone to sleep, though nobody on the other boats had ever told us about this. Now the snapper were ready to party.

Minutes later each of us had his own 20-plus-pound snapper flopping on the deck. It was unbelievable. And what happened next will stay with me forever. A world record snapper will probably never be caught on my boat, and I'm not listed in the IGFA. But there are few anglers who can say they've cranked up a two-hook bottom rig, with a pair of red snappers attached, that weighed 27 and 28 pounds. I've caught a lot of great fish in my life, from marlin on down, but 55 pounds of snapper on one drop was more than enough to make me a bottom fisherman for life.

GARY FOLDEN

Armed only with light spinning gear and a livewell filled with scaled sardines, I was out scouting the shallow Gulf for silver trout in autumn.

That reconnaissance mission produced nary a trout, so, running the boat about a mile off the beach, I was making the 7-mile run back to Clearwater. I had the fishfinder turned on, thank goodness, and was watching the gentle variation of bottom contours. A sudden and quick change in depth caught my eye. I slowed the boat and reversed course, to investigate this bottom "anomaly."

It appeared to be a coral ledge. Had I found some rock in 18 feet of water that might be holding silver trout? I anchored the boat, then flipped a sardine out on the light tackle, with a split shot attached. That bait barely made bottom before something devoured it, as well as cutting me off. Two more drops met with the same fate. What was down there? With only the light spinning tackle on board, I quickly located a spool of 50-pound leader material, and wound on 25 feet of heavy line. While tightening the drag, I lowered down another bait. Once again the live sardine met with a jarring strike.

In a little over an hour I landed five gag grouper from my new spot, with the largest at 12 pounds. A very pleasant surprise. Prowling the area on future trips, I found there was actually a six-acre parcel of hard bottom associated with that original rockpile. Only a mile

Gary Folden adjusts his bottom machine while circling one of his favorite grouper spots.

off a beach named Sand Key, it lay tucked away with several other grouper spots in that same hard bottom region. In the years to follow, I caught many large gag grouper from those spots.

I soon noticed that large king mackerel were also abundant in this same six acres, in addition to the grouper, snapper, seabass and triggerfish. In an attempt to keep it to myself, I tried many tricks to keep this little section of the Gulf a secret. It worked for nearly four years before I was finally "caught" there.

Nearly two decades later, this small patch in the Gulf of Mexico is now known on fishing charts as the famous "Hard bottom off Sand Key." Every spring and fall it's hard to imagine how many kingfish boats crowd together on this little spot during the big tournaments.

I rarely fish there now because of the number of boats that stop, but finding that first ledge and having it all to myself was one of the best birthday presents ever. Now, just as you'll do, I keep a lookout for my next honeyhole.

GEORGE MITCHELL

When bottom fishing, you should never give up out there, and always fish like it's your last day. You never know what is lurking down there...

I can recall a day out on the reef, drift-fishing our live baits deep. However, an October north wind had scared the mullet out of their usual haunts. I must have thrown the 12-foot castnet a dozen times, before we had our first bait. Two long hours later we had a grand total of eight live mullet, and it was time to fish or give it up. News on the VHF radio wasn't good at all; a lot of kingfish had suddenly appeared, making things very difficult for the sailfish fleet. Our chances of catching grouper and snapper seemed to be shrinking by the minute.

We decided to power drift over a natural ledge in 140 feet. We used just one rod, a 2-speed, 50-pound outfit filled with 50-pound superline. We added a stinger hook with wire, in case a kingfish tried to steal

George Mitchell and Jenny Simmons with her first black grouper.

bottom rod for another try.

the bait. I motored upcurrent of the spot and opened the livewell for a mullet. To my surprise, one jumped clear of the boat. Down to seven baits!

We both then huddled over the livewell and scooped up a dandy, pinning a 5/0 hook through his lips, with the stinger hook farther back. Nellie, my fishing partner for the day, lowered the bait deep. I noted some big fish marks on the bottom machine and spun around, but Nellie was already hooked up, the rodtip bent to the water. It was a 28-pound black grouper.

After landing the fish and giving a high-five, we motored back for another drift. I was feeling good, but not thinking good. I opened the bait door, and another mullet clears the transom! Down to five baits...So we huddled around the livewell, scooped out another mullet, and reloaded the bottom rod. Wham! Nellie was bowed over again and the battle was on. This time, a 21-pound mutton snapper was lifted aboard with the gaff.

By now we knew the game: guard the livewell, and get every mullet on the hook. And our next drop was the day's best, a 38-pound black grouper. The last three mullet were slammed by a pair of 12-pound muttons and another black grouper tipping the scales at 16 pounds.

That action took place in less than two hours, if you discount work with the castnet. It was all over by noon, and we had the best catch of the year for our fishing club. More than once that day, I had suggested we let the baits go free, and skip to a better day. We were both so glad we hung in there... As for the two mullet that got away, we're not sure, but while battling the second grouper, we saw a kingfish skyrocket with what looked like our number eight mullet in his mouth.

It's the memory of that day and others not quite so good that keep me coming back to bottom fish the reef country, through bad weather, scarce bait, and all the rest of the obstacles life can deal us. SB

SNAPPER FACTS

> Live in water from 2 to 1,000 feet
> Prefer smaller, less prickly baits
> More particular than grouper
> Usually red, but always colorful

GROUPER FACTS

> Bigger mouths than snapper
> Gulp their meals
> Don't mind prickly baits
> Often brown, many are colorful

CHAPTER 1

SNAPPER & GROUPER

E ver try to turn down a baked snapper, or fried grouper fingers? Not many have, and the multitude of anglers who pursue these fish have one thing in common, they like to eat what they catch. Folks who rely on restaurants and fish markets for their fish diet often have no idea what truly fresh fish tastes like. Often, the only way to find out is to catch these fish yourself. Or hang around your neighbor's front yard when his boat returns from another successful trip offshore.

Meet the Players

Fishermen devote a great deal of time learning the tricks of their trade, in finding snapper and grouper. We've got them lined up for you here, and we've included every trick in the book. This book, anyway. Every species of snapper and grouper worth pursuing, even some of the rare ones. From two feet of water out to 1,000 feet. In the Gulf of Mexico and the South Atlantic states. Even a few islands in other countries.

Catching a mix of quality snapper and grouper on the same spot is always fun. Note the snell-rigged hook, making for good hook-set.

Snapper and grouper can be caught with just about any tackle, but there are plenty of tricks to the trade.

The Snapper Family

Gray Snapper
Red Snapper
Mutton Snapper
Lane Snapper
Cubera Snapper
Dog Snapper
Schoolmaster Snapper
Yellowtail Snapper

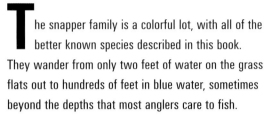

Vermilion Snapper
Mahogany Snapper
Blackfin Snapper
Silk Snapper
Queen Snapper

The snapper family is a colorful lot, with all of the better known species described in this book. They wander from only two feet of water on the grass flats out to hundreds of feet in blue water, sometimes beyond the depths that most anglers care to fish.

We've targeted the top three snapper species (red, mutton and mangrove) on the next few pages for an in-depth look, and saved the remainder for last. The remainder are broken up into four major groups, each grouped by the depth of water they prefer, to better remember them. Each is unique and quite tasty on the fork, which explains some of their popularity.

The four major snapper groups are current feeders, reef snapper, bad boys and deep-drop snapper. Current feeders stay relatively high above bottom, feeding on smaller organisms as they pass by in the current. Reef snappers are the colorful clan that stick close to coral reefs during the day, often feeding more at night. The term "bad boys" is meant to describe two of the snappers that grow large, and carry fang-like teeth that are capable of inflicting a nasty bite to prey and fishermen alike. Last are the deep-drop snappers that spend their time from 500 to beyond 1,000 feet down, in the cold blue water offshore. Catching them is a different ballgame entirely.

Red snapper milling around on bottom structure offshore are fair game for fishermen, especially on the crowded weekends.

TOP THREE SNAPPER

① **RED SNAPPER**

② **MANGROVE SNAPPER**

③ **MUTTON SNAPPER**

Mutton snapper prefer much more tropical settings, southern latitudes and coral reefs.

If it weren't for the "top three" species listed here, snapper fishing in U.S. waters would be relegated to a pretty minor role. These three fish are the main players.

Red and mutton snapper grow to 30 pounds and they're almost identical in shape and nearly so in color. When the range of one runs out, the other takes over. The red snapper is a northern fish, venturing as far as North Carolina. The southern cousin is the mutton snapper, a fish that prefers tropical settings and coral reefs.

The little cousin, found almost anywhere in warm, shallow water, is the gray or mangrove snapper, nicknamed "mango" for short. The smartest of all snapper, they use their wits to survive even in clear marina harbors.

MANGROVE

MUTTON

RED

The commercial fishing industry pursued red snapper stocks to all corners of the Gulf.

The Snapper Family

① RED SNAPPER

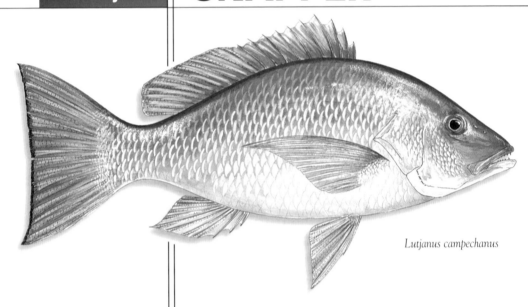

Lutjanus campechanus

If we're going to discuss bottom fishing in six Southern coastal states, including Florida, we have to start with the American red snapper. Whether it's their beautiful color, great fighting ability, lofty status among fishermen, or just the incredible way they grace a cooking grill, no bottom fish can challenge this queen of the reef.

Populations of red snapper were beaten down after a century of commercial fishing, but the good news is that fisheries management measures have done an amazing job of not only rebuilding stocks in their traditional haunts, but also expanding the red snapper's range. Gulf anglers are now finding red snapper in areas where not even the old-timers can remember seeing them. On the Atlantic side, they're releasing lots of fine, 20-inch snapper, fish that were quite rare in the early 1990s. Some of the boats are limiting out on 8- to 12-pound snapper, with occasional fish up to 28 pounds.

Red snapper can be caught on just about any rod and reel with enough line to reach bottom, on any bait from stinky squid to expensive, live goggle-eyes. There are plenty of tricks to the trade, however. It's best to learn the basics, fish a number of spots, and keep good records of the trip. With a little practice, you'll have that

QUEEN OF THE REEF

The popularity of red snapper is very high, and for good reason. They're a beautiful red color, easy to identify, have a distinctively fine flavor on the table, fight hard, and will often bite on days when most grouper won't. Most reds are caught in the Gulf of Mexico from Port St. Joe, Florida, west all the way to Texas, in depths from 60 to 200 feet. However, the Atlantic coast has seen a resurgence of these fish, from Cape Canaveral north into Georgia waters.

❶ RED SNAPPER

beautiful red color lining your fishbox on just about every trip. Many of the chapters in this book deal with different aspects of catching red snapper.

The best natural bottom on Florida's Atlantic coast stretches from Fernandina Beach south to St. Augustine. This region

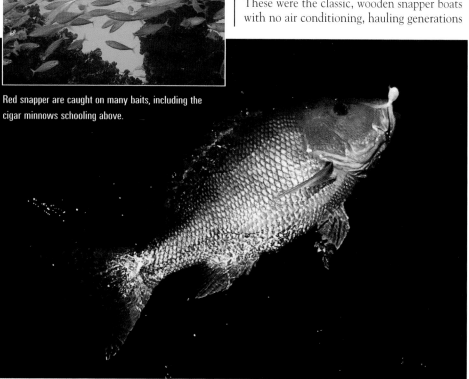

Red snapper are caught on many baits, including the cigar minnows schooling above.

tyboats out of Mayport (Jacksonville) alone. Weather permitting. Red snapper have propped up the partyboat industry since its inception, as they were easy to catch for many years, using early tackle that is considered a bit primitive by today's standards.

Similar conditions exist in the northern Gulf, where snapper fishing really got started in the early 1900s. By 1915 there were at least 11 boats for hire out of Panama City alone, with a capacity for 40 to 100 anglers each. These were the classic, wooden snapper boats with no air conditioning, hauling generations

includes dozens of sizeable areas within 30 miles of the coast, with either limestone ledges or the live coral bottom these fish prefer. This is natural bottom heaven for local anglers; long before anyone thought about sinking ships to create artificial reefs, Northeast Florida was widely known to have the best red snapper fishery on America's Atlantic Coast. More than 50 years ago, at least 200 people per day were fishing on par-

of sweaty fishermen, new and old, out to what were then called the "snapper banks." Back then you filled a "grass" or "tow sack" with a hundred pounds of snapper on a good day. That all depended on just how adept the captain was at finding good bottom, without benefit of modern electronics. Some captains made it look easy, and some days it was.

Today, the Gulf coastline from Florida to Texas is home to hundreds of charterboats,

Horsing up big snapper on heavy tackle isn't for the weak of heart. Sometimes it takes strong encouragement.

and thousands of recreational boats, whose captains and crews spend the majority of their fishing time pursuing red snapper, gag grouper, black (mangrove) snapper and other assorted bottom fish. Alabama and western Florida counties have aggressive artificial reef programs. With so many anglers on the water today, most believe the new reefs have been critical in supplying fish-attracting bottom structure, on a sandy and mostly featureless bottom in that area of the Gulf.

There are, of course, big ledges and rockpiles in the northern Gulf, where 50-pound "copperbelly" gags and giant warsaw grouper still roam and ravage tackle. However, for the average coastal angler dropping baits off Panhandle Florida, it is the inshore wrecks and artificial reefs that give up most of the quality bottom fish.

Anglers on the Florida Panhandle have much in common with Northeast Florida anglers on the Atlantic. They both enjoy access to great red snapper fishing, and both are heavily dependent today on artificial reefs. Between them there is a difference, however. It seems that Pensacola has the honorable distinction of giving up 15-pound red snapper from artificial reefs inside the bay itself. That hasn't happened yet on the East Coast and probably never will, but the two fisheries have so much in common, we've dealt with them equally throughout this book.

The red snapper isn't too picky. They take a huge variety of baits, and they don't mind jigs tipped with something sweet.

A Century of Pursuing Snapper

The red is still the mightiest of all snapper, numbers wise, supporting an unrestricted, multi-million pound commercial fishery for more than a century. Pensacola's early sail and then motorized commercial snapper fleet was built to "prosecute" (as they used to say) this huge fishery, with large, sail-driven vessels prowling the Gulf. Stocks near Pensacola were quickly impacted, followed by the Florida Middle Grounds, Dry Tortugas, and lastly, the big Campeche Banks off Mexico. These vessels often returned to port with their full load of 40,000 pounds of snapper (with some grouper) on board, after a month-long voyage. This is a non-sophisticated fish; for many years they were caught with handline alone. Crews often used barrels of salted ladyfish for bait. Their boats wandered evey corner of the Gulf from the late 1800s until about 1960, when red snapper stocks fell too low to support such major efforts. During that period, millions of pounds were shipped around the country by railroad, using ice alone, before refrigeration.

Today, with strict management and closed seasons, red snapper stocks are rebuilding. Charterboats out of Pensacola are now limiting out on good-sized snapper in only three hours of fishing. This continues despite the fact that a great many recreational boats are equipped with ultra-modern fish-finding equipment. Bottom-scouring nets from trawling shrimpboats have also wasted countless small red snapper, but that is another story, saved for the conservation chapter. SB

Big mangrove snapper are a real prize. Most of the bigger ones are caught at night.

❷ MANGROVE SNAPPER

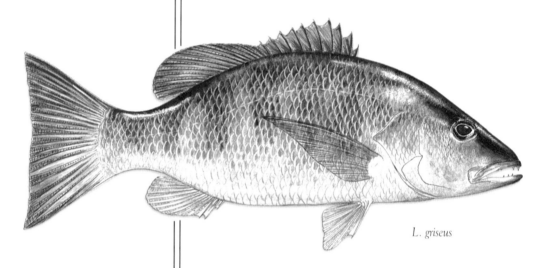

L. griseus

The darling of all Florida snappers, the gray (or commonly called mangrove, or black) snapper is found everywhere, providing food and sport for all anglers—even kids fishing from marina docks. This neighborhood fish also happens to be very good table fare, adding to its popularity.

The best part is you won't need offshore weather to catch a mess of mangroves, because many of their habitats are sheltered from strong winds. These guys can be found from twisting mangrove tidal creeks in the Everglades, to freshwater rivers and springs, canals, marina harbors, and jetties—and then beyond, out to depths of 120 feet and more offshore. They swarm the hilly Middle Grounds 80 miles off the coast of Tampa, almost all sunken wrecks from Tampa south, any mangrove trees with a root system in salty or brackish water, various creeks and harbors, bridges and jetties. They're everyman's fish.

Water temperatures will dictate where these fish are found, since they have a disdain for cold water. The best time of year to target them is early to midsummer, when they spawn during the full moons of May, June and July. They're also supposed to have a smaller spawn during the full moons of October and November.

As their name implies, they're quite fond of mangrove trees skirting coastal bays and channel edges. It's the perfect habitat for younger fish, who grow up and begin to explore. They finally work their way out

DID YOU KNOW?

The mangrove snapper is possibly the smartest of all fish in the sea. Around docks and marinas, they're amazingly quick to learn, and they can spot a tiny hook hidden inside a bait. Their cousins from the backcountry aren't quite so smart, and they'll hit a topwater plug in broad daylight, in isolated mangrove creeks that see little fishing pressure. Either way, they're always a sporty fish.

to the shallow reefs, and then deeper reefs, ledges and wrecks. As long as the water temperature suits them.

A very opportunistic fish, mangrove "dock snappers" can be found under almost any fish cleaning table in Florida. These fish are extremely smart—the PhD's of the aquatic world. You might be able to fool one of them into biting, but once his brethren see him struggle, the remainder become very tight-lipped.

If you want to learn what actually happens when a mangrove snapper eats your bait, spend some time watching them under a dock. Drop a few baits overboard and watch how they eat:

Using their canine teeth, these fish will impale the bait a few times before swallowing. With a live shrimp, they'll almost always bite it in the middle, then dart away to swallow it. Perhaps they suspect a hook at one end of the shrimp or the other.

May, June and July are best for catching the bigger, deeper mangroves offshore. This is mainly night-time action, or fishing at sundown and into the night. These fish usually begin to congregate perhaps a week before the full moon of May, and continue spawning until the end of July. Best bet here is to find a natural ledge in the 30- to 60-foot depths. Stuart

When these fish hear noise, they want to see what's up. (Maybe dinner.)

and Fort Lauderdale in Southeast Florida offer reefs at these depths that can be great, for instance. Marine researchers at Tequesta Research Center have found that mangrove snapper even feed on small sea turtles in that area during summer, somehow snatching hatchling turtles from the surface in 120 feet of water. To locate these bigger and more aggressive snappers, anchor over rough or rocky bottom and try chumming, *especially* at night.

When you decide where you're going to fish for mangroves, figure out how wind and current will affect the boat. If it's a ledge or a pothole in a channel, try to approach from upcur-

Backcountry mangroves are more apt to slash at topwater plugs, since they're not used to fishing pressure.

rent so you don't motor over the prime area. Once anchored correctly, start thinking like a snapper. Mangroves are inquisitive fish; when they hear engine noise, they want to see what's up. (Maybe dinner.) They will leave the safety of their ambush spot to find out what's making the noise. However, sudden, loud sounds after the engine is shut off can kill a fishing trip here. There's nothing to be gained by slamming a livewell hatch, or dropping pliers. A little stealth goes a long way.

Mangrove snapper are the key targets of anglers fishing the Gulf Middle Grounds at night. The area swarms with these fish, but they're smart enough to evade a hook during the day. That means night fishing, preferably under moonlight. Bigger mangroves up to 10 pounds are invariably caught at night, and they're a tough fish to stop with lighter tackle. They certainly have a knack for ducking into rocks or under ledges when given half a chance.

This night-time action is the same in the Florida Keys, and that's often why anglers spend the night offshore, or at least fish a few hours after dark. Off Key West, you can load up on night-time mangroves and still make the scene downtown while the bands are playing. (Not so on the Middle Grounds.)

For night action, the trick is to load up the spin tackle with 25-pound line, the typical sliding egg weight and 40-pound leader, perhaps fluorocarbon, which is hard to see underwater. Bring a variety of baits (see the bait chapter) and a fair amount of chum, and have some fun. These fish fight hard for their size, and fooling a big one is an accomplishment. It's a great way to spend an evening, and there isn't the slightest chance of getting a sunburn.

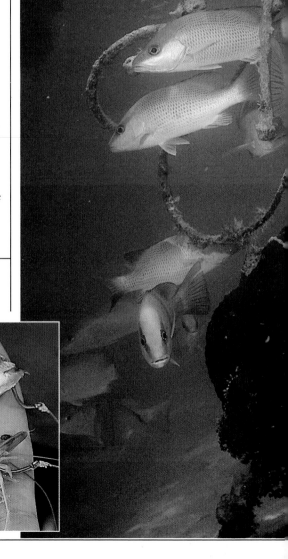

Key baits for mangroves are lively pinfish and big, live shrimp.

The Darling of Shore Fishermen

The gray snapper (*L. griseus*) is everybody's favorite shallow water snapper. Often called mangrove snapper, they'll hide and feed around mangrove tree roots in tropical tidal creeks. Easily the smartest of all snapper, those found around marina docks seemingly have more intelligence than their backcountry cousins. These fish will eat nine free shrimp, and turn their noses up at the tenth, that has a small hook cleverly hidden inside on 6-pound line. It's enough to drive some anglers crazy. In the northern Gulf, they're called "black snapper," because they're somewhat darker than more numerous red snapper. They also feed at mid-depth offshore, high above the snapper rocks, a cautious fish that is difficult to catch.

This is another snapper that, if you want to fool the bigger ones, your best chance is at night. During daylight, live bait is normally the ticket. However, in far-flung, tropical waters these guys may hit a jig, spoon, even a topwater plug, in broad daylight. Bigger specimens move offshore, growing to 15 pounds and perhaps a little more, and spend their lives around rocks and wrecks out to at least 100 feet. An opportunistic fish, they'll cruise or hover 50 feet above a wreck, picking up bait and chum, especially those tidbits that don't have a line attached.

They're also super-quick, popping their jaws when caught, and many an angler has been shocked when a gray snapper clamped down on the nearest piece of human anatomy—and refused to turn loose. SB

A nice colony of mangrove snapper roams for food beneath a deepwater dock.

Trophy mutton snapper taken at night in a Bahamas harbor. The fish struck a plug.

❸ MUTTON SNAPPER

L. analis

Down in South Florida, mutton snappers have always been a favorite; they're big, beautiful and can be caught year-round. Scattered throughout the Caribbean and Bahamas, their range is limited in U.S. waters, and only wraps around Florida from Cape Canaveral on the east coast, through the Keys, then up to the Middle Grounds off Tampa. Although the majority of muttons today are caught in deeper water, they do inhabit shallower "patch" coral reefs, as well as channels and creeks connecting ocean to bays. Big muttons can also be found prowling the grassflats, often while following stingrays in the shallows. It's a wonderful sight to see, though not as common as years ago.

Location for muttons is everything. In winter you can find plenty on shallow wrecks and natural coral reefs in less than 40 feet of water. Farther north in the Palm Beach area, they can be found in some dredge holes just off the beach, and even on some of the shallower artificial reefs made of concrete. They're more commonly found on deeper artificial wrecks and reefs. South of the Dade-Broward county line and into the Keys, they seem to prefer live coral over everything else. That does not mean some of the wrecks in 150 to 200 feet

DID YOU KNOW?

> Mutton snapper roam warmer waters in southern latitudes, and won't tolerate sharp drops in temperatures.

> The Bahamas and Caribbean are far more suitable habitat for muttons, but they are commonly found in the Florida Keys.

> Ten-pound muttons and larger are capable of roaming grassflats in only two feet of water, where they can be caught on a fly rod.

aren't hot with muttons, however.

Near Miami and to the south are plenty of live coral "patch" reefs, often visible from the surface, and the winter mutton fishery there

Prime baits for offshore muttons include butterflied baits at top, heads, chunks, and local live baits.

can be great. That action would include adjacent finger channels leading into Biscayne Bay.

Your best bet is to do a little homework and put together a game plan where you want to

Mutton snapper also roam out to 200 feet and slightly more.

fish. Listen to local fish reports, pick some good bottom, and also the right time to go. The moon phase doesn't really matter, but the tides certainly do. Look for a day with good tidal flow.

During spring, the shallow patch reefs and dredge holes provide good habitat for muttons,

due to an abundance of small pilchards and herring. This is another area where the tide and wind should ideally work together. You can fish both these areas the same way, except for the bait process. Almost every patch reef will hold live ballyhoo, while very few dredge holes do. When fishing dredge holes, it may be easier to fill the livewell with pilchards, and use them to chum the snappers close.

Patch reefs can be fished in the same manner as the dredge holes or maybe with live ballyhoo, and this can be spectacular. Experts have had days where they've caught as many as 15 legal-sized muttons on these shallower reefs, and never had to pull anchor except to "head for the house." Patch reefs can be good year-round, but the best months are almost always between November and February, when the reefs are loaded with winter ballyhoo.

Many mutton snapper today are taken in slightly deeper water, meaning 100 to 200 feet. Some boats anchor on these deeper wrecks or small reefs, waiting out the muttons. Some of the veteran captains much prefer drifting, covering new ground, until they hit the day's hotspot. Repeated drifts in the same spot often pick up additional fish.

The drift technique entails dropping a combination of live baits deep, as the boat drifts over a sunken wreck or artificial reef of some sort, including concrete material. (Both are the top two reef materials). A sloping live bottom with sea fans and other soft marine growth is also good.

Boat captains drift the boat sideways to a gentle breeze or current, spreading out three or four anglers with their lines from bow to stern, to prevent tangling. On faster drift days they may "motor fish," which means slowing down the drift or even stopping it for moments on end, especially over small reefs. They do this by backing the boat's engines into the waves every half minute or so, as needed. (Boats with high transoms are recommended for this work). Two anglers are stationed in the stern near the livewell, and they're responsible for keeping their lines out of the propellers. Remaining anglers drop their lines from the bow.

"Muttonfish" Have So Many Fans

This tropical beauty has more subtle coloring than the red snapper. Fish taken from deeper water have an overall pinkish hue, while those near shallow water have a greenish back with red fins and pink belly. That beckoning, red tail color in only two feet of water on far South Florida grassflats is the ultimate prize for many flyrod anglers. Though not nearly as common in the shallows as they once were, catching a mutton in thin water remains a viable, rewarding quest for flyrod anglers.

A fish that versatile, prowling grassflats and channels, coral reefs and deeper water, is bound to succeed in the face of tough fishing pressure. Perfectly content in Bahamian or Caribbean mangrove tidal creeks and shallow coral, these guys hang around wrecks, reefs and rocks out to 200 feet and deeper. They'll strike a jig, plug or spoon as well as the fly, which makes them a sporty proposition. Found anywhere south of Tampa, this is the main go-to snapper in clear, tropical waters of this hemisphere.

Here's a trophy of the trip: In a mangrove creek in Belize, a fine mutton snapper that crashed a topwater plug, a brokenback minnow.

On the table? There's been many a sunburned angler who's taken a bite of his baked "muttonfish," rolled his eyes and sighed, "Sweet Mother of Mercy." Well, at least fishermen of Irish descent have, but you get the picture. Photo courtesy of Pete Churton. SB

❸ MUTTON SNAPPER

A livewell full of pinfish, castnetted bally-hoo or scaled sardines is advisable, since muttons favor something flashy or alive. That's why mutton veterans spend an hour or two hunting prime bait each morning, checking their pinfish traps, and then castnetting for sardine species. Failing that, they drop sabiki rigs near the buoys and towers offshore. Almost any flashy, hard-wiggling bait in the 3- to 5-inch range has a shot at

Shallow water muttons have green backs, while deeper fish, like this one taken in 160 feet, have pink backs.

Muttons will also pursue artificials trolled deep near bottom.

catching a mutton snapper.

Muttons will also pursue baits and artificials trolled deep near bottom. With today's wide range of trolling plugs that can be fine-tuned (with braided line) to wiggle down to 50 feet, more mutton snapper will likely be caught with this technique. Of course, finding muttons in that depth is the first step. In The Bahamas and Caribbean, with far less fishing pressure, muttons can commonly be found in easy range of today's generation of diving plugs. So, it's a wise choice to carry a few big plugs there as insurance.

Many Bahamians seldom fish for muttons on the reefs, but prefer to fish the grassflats between the patch reefs of coral. Trolling from coral head to head or to your next destination may be your best bet at finding a few large muttons.

Here we loosely classify other snappers into four categories.

CURRENT FEEDERS

These are a different genera of snapper, wearing scientific names that distinguish them from other members of the Lutjanidae family. They're built and look quite different from the rest. They hang around coral reefs, but feed much higher in the water column, catching small organisms as they drift by in the current. Both have small mouths, so a small hook and

lighter tackle are usually advisable. Both remain in good number, when bag limits are implemented to protect them. Curiously, they also don't seem to cross each other's turf very often. The vermilion is a northern fish (North Florida to North Carolina, and the Upper Gulf of Mexico), while the yellowtail prefers tropical waters.

REEF SNAPPERS

Reef snappers are the standard-shaped (Lutjanus) snappers so familiar to the public. These fish are perfectly happy hugging bottom, often around shallow coral reefs accessible even to children. Reef snappers school up against or lurk beneath coral heads, and always seem to be waiting for something to happen. At least that is their demeanor, when studied by underwater observers. With the exception of mangrove snapper, these fish are not picky and will

often feed on almost anything small and palatable. They're not so shy of hooks and leaders, and can be caught in the daytime. They've provided many a meal for fishermen in tropical waters, who would have had a meal of only rice and beans instead.

BAD BOYS

The Bad Boys is our nickname for the two fiercest-looking snappers, fish that have large canine teeth capable of grabbing and holding large prey. One of these, the cubera snapper, reaches 150 pounds, a brute that can easily crush whole lobsters into mush. That's the rec-

ommended live bait for those who pursue cuberas. This is a fish that really gets around, hitting trolled live baits on occasion, sometimes on the surface. The cubera and its cousin, the dog snapper, favor reefs and wrecks and are top predators. Both school in spawning aggregations and can be targeted at historic gathering sites, usually during the full moon in September. Both are suspect in cases involving ciguatera, and can now be tested with a portable kit for presence of the toxin.

DEEP-DROP

The Deep-Drop snappers don't prowl over bottom quite as deep as some in the grouper family, but they still live deeper than many anglers ever bother to fish. With advances in deep-drop fishing gear, usually involving electric reels and small lights that attach to the leaders, many anglers have found it enjoyable to spend at least an hour making these drops, dur-

ing a long day spent off-shore. Trolling for pelagics isn't always productive, so it's good insurance to carry this specialized bottom gear along during the day. Cranking up a string of (up to) six silk snapper in one drop is a sure way to provide a fresh dinner for the family. Deeper water also holds a mystery, and one never knows what sort of fish may be brought up.

Yellowtail

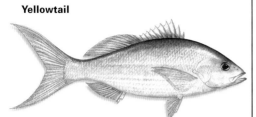

Vermilion

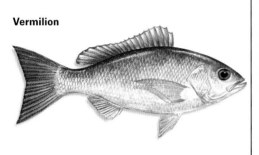

Two shallow-water snappers swarm high in the water column, feeding on small tidbits that pass by in the current. They will also hit some sizeable baits meant for bigger fish.

YELLOWTAIL SNAPPER
Ocyurus chrysurus

Colorful, sporty on light tackle, certainly quite tasty, the yellowtail perseveres where coral reefs, offshore sandbars and tropical rocks can be found. Big "flags" up to five pounds and more can be taken, mostly by chumming these fish at night. In the clear, clean waters around coral reefs, the sharp-eyed yellowtail sometimes won't even take a hook during daylight hours. But at night? Anchor up and chum; drop some sand balls overboard, the sand mixed together with glass minnows, cooked oatmeal and a squirt of menhaden oil. Feed a small, unweighted bait back in the current on lighter tackle, and watch what happens!

Fishing for yellowtail is a sport all by itself, but it's relegated to wherever coral reefs can be found. That pretty much restricts the U.S. fishery from Miami down to the Florida Keys. Farther south and in The Bahamas, they're quite numerous. A welcome guest at the table, because they're delicious.

VERMILION SNAPPER
Rhomboplites aurorubens

Another crowd pleaser, vermilions swarm above the rocks 20 and 30 feet above bottom, almost anywhere north of yellowtail country. Often called "beeliners," they're not big; a 3- or 4-pounder instead might be called "ocean liner." When strict limits were handed down for red snapper, it was the beeliner that took up the slack. Without bag limits, folks were happy to fill the box with these smaller fish, often only 10 inches long. The pressure grew until a 10-fish limit was finally necessary in Atlantic waters. Since they have such a small mouth, it's best to use small but strong circle hooks, and small chunks of fresh squid. They'll bite on heavy tackle even in broad daylight, but bigger specimens seem more easily caught at night, sometimes two and three at a time on multi-hook rigs.

Yellowtail snapper have the classic forked tail of current feeders, as do vermilion snapper, below.

REEF SNAPPERS

SCHOOLMASTER SNAPPER
L. apodus

These are small, yellow and brown snapper seen hovering around shallow coral reefs in only eight feet of water, sometimes in small schools. Not even remotely as smart as the gray snapper, the schoolmaster will pick up small baits of many kinds, in daylight hours. They're very dependable, great for small kids to catch, and have that good snapper taste on the table. This is probably the easiest of all

Schoolmaster

Lane snapper

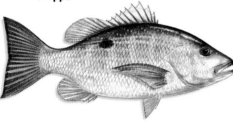

Mahogany

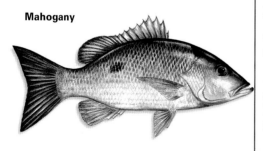

snappers to catch. Unfortunately, they seldom grow over 14 inches. They have, however, been baked over many an open cooking fire on the beach down in the tropical latitudes, and no one has complained.

LANE SNAPPER *L. synagris*

Not nearly as numerous as some of the others, notably the gray. They're sometimes called "candy snapper" because of the fine, yellow lines running through a red body. They're almost identical to red snapper, except for those yellow shades. They also mix with red snapper, and a headboat fishing the Gulf, its crew cranking up red snapper all day, will likely see a handful of lane snapper as well. The lanes have never been as numerous as the reds, for some reason, except in isolated places. The lane also wanders into shallow, grassy bottom, unlike the red.

Lanes will hit the same cut baits that catch red snapper on the bottom, and they sometimes have a reputation for having slightly softer meat than the red. For this reason, they may not freeze quite as well, and should be eaten fresh if possible.

MAHOGANY SNAPPER
L. mahogoni

Rare in U.S. waters, this fish is only seen on coral reefs in far South Florida and the Keys. Most are caught in The Bahamas and Caribbean. They favor very salty water and seem to avoid freshwater runoff if at all possible, so that makes them scarce off most southern coastal states. This is a shallow-water snapper, shaped somewhat like the gray snapper, but thinner. The mahogany is more colorful; reddish dorsal fin and tail, fiery red eyes, and a silvery belly. These fish only grow to about 20 inches, but they're a favorite down in the islands, because they swim in good-sized schools, hovering around coral heads. Those big eyes are rather unusual for shallow water fish.

Fast action on smaller reef snappers can be found in fairly shallow water, on the right tides. It helps if a coral reef can be found and anchored over. Matching lighter tackle to these fish is the ticket here. Above is a lane snapper and below, a schoolmaster.

CUBERA SNAPPERS *L. cyanopterus*

The sheer size of adult cubera snapper is enough to make most anglers pause. Here is a snapper that grows to at least 150 pounds on occasion. Farther offshore, who knows? Underwater they look like a huge grouper, perhaps a goliath grouper, but the canine fangs quickly give them away as being a cubera.

A secretive fish, most big cuberas are targeted in July and August, when they gather to spawn around certain deeper wrecks during the full moon, down in the Florida Keys. The trick here is to drop a live, legal-sized lobster down, perhaps pinned to a heavy jig with a stinger hook, and slug it out with them on sturdy tackle. These fish run hard, diving for cover, even careening through underwater coral canyons, and the fight is brutal. Most cuberas in this scenario average from 40 to 80 pounds each.

Smaller cuberas from 10 to 30 pounds can be found in tidal creeks, often with six or eight fish peering out from undercut creek banks in places like Belize. A live grunt suspended under a cork will work here. It has been surmised that, since occasional big cuberas are found all over the Gulf, but small ones aren't, that the adult fish are true wanderers. They're also a worthy adversary. Consumption of bigger specimens has been linked to ciguatera poi-

soning, because they're apex reef predators. However, a test kit can now be carried on boats, with a tiny piece of fish fin serving as a sample. If the fish tests positive, they can be released. As they should be.

Smaller cuberas are good on the table, especially when stuffed with lobster meat. Bigger specimens are probably tougher to eat.

DOG SNAPPERS *L. jocu*

Another tough species, this snapper grows to 20 pounds or so. These guys do favor coral reefs more than other structure, and so have been implicated with more than a few ciguatera poisoning cases. Built solid and very chunky, the dog snapper sports an impressive set of fangs, much like the cubera. At least one fang is visible, even when the mouth is closed. Not a picky feeder, they'll grab just about any kind of bait, even jigs. Since they're found around coral, this pretty much relegates them to the Caribbean Sea and The Bahamas. Some are found in the Florida Keys as well, and the younger specimens can often be seen hovering around coral heads in fairly shallow water.

Cubera

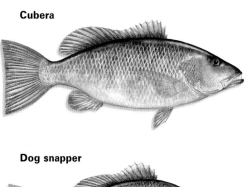

Dog snapper

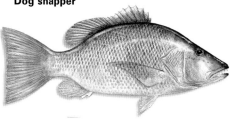

With their sharp fangs and nasty disposition, cubera and dog snappers are always a thrill to catch. They're top reef predators for the snapper family, often feeding on lobster. Cubera at right was caught in a mangrove creek next to a deep, undercut bank. Above, a 10-pound dog snapper hunts for a meal. Both were photographed in Belize.

DEEP-DROP SNAPPERS

SILK SNAPPER *L. vivanus*

Of the four deepwater species, silks seem the most prevalent. They can easily be picked out in a fish market. They're the posted "red snapper" with the yellow eyes, and the familiar snapper body. That makes them a silk snapper.

Silkies favor deeper rocks and pinnacles, feeding on fresh, cut bait (blue runner or blackfin tuna fillet is good, or squid), lowered down from 300 to a reported 720 feet on electric reels. While 18 pounds is about tops, the average silk is a solid six to eight pounds in some areas, making them a worthy prize. In other areas, small silkies are the norm. The trick is to drop a few circle hooks down and drift over favorable bottom, cranking up every 10 minutes or so. On the right drop, one angler may bring up from three to five of these fish. In the Gulf, they can sometimes be taken even on the 30-fathom rocks if a substantial dropoff is close by. This is very similar to bottom fishing for red snapper, except the water is deeper. As a bonus for cranking them up from so deep, they are considered by some to be the most flavorful of all snapper.

QUEEN SNAPPER *E. oculatus*

All snapper species are one of a kind, but queens are special. They're long, slender, a beautiful red fish, yellow eyes with a deeply forked tail. They hang around the deep, big rocks (the size of houses) in 600 to 1,000 feet of water, so anglers can forget about anchoring their boat. On days when the current is very slow, it's possible to drop a heavy weight that far down, hooks baited with chunks of fish. The queen grows to at least three feet long, and doesn't get much fishing pressure, except deepwater trapping in The Bahamas. Why? Commercial bottom longlines can't handle rocky bottom, nobody can anchor over these fish, so it is the brief drift, the equivalent of a "drive-by," that catches a few of these trophy fish. They're also quite good to eat.

BLACKFIN SNAPPER *L. buccanella*

Another deepwater fish, ranging down to 650 feet. This is a stocky snapper that only grows to a reported length of 16 inches, but a possible four pounds. Unconfirmed stories from commercial fishermen tell of blackfins weighing up to 30 pounds, caught in Tongue of the Ocean off Andros Island. That place has a reputation for very deep water and unusually mild currents, so that may be the place to catch a world record blackfin. Though they may be strong fighters, it's hard to tell when hooking them so far below, when heavier tackle is often required to drop baits and weights so deep.

Often confused with red snapper, the blackfin has yellow eyes and a black crescent on its pectoral fins. They love the deep dropoffs near the continental shelf in the Gulf, Caribbean and The Bahamas. While the younger fish are sometimes taken in only 100-200 feet, the adults prowl *much* deeper.

Silk snapper

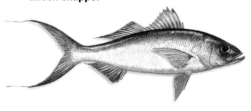

Queen snapper

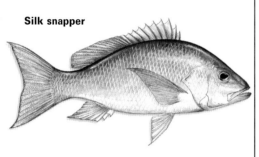

Blackfin snapper

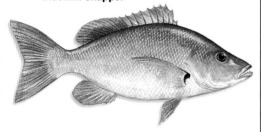

Dropping a bait 3 to10 times deeper than many people have ever fished isn't something done lightly. Even reaching *bottom* with the baits can be a problem, let alone cranking the fish up. Some anglers try to catch state record fish without electrics, to qualify for the rod and reel division. Most people use electric equipment, though it is less sporty. Above, a silk snapper. Below is a queen snapper.

The Grouper Family

Gag Grouper
Black Grouper
Yellowfin Grouper
Scamp
Yellowmouth Grouper
Tiger Grouper
Goliath Grouper
Warsaw Grouper
Red Grouper
Nassau Grouper
Red Hind
Rock Hind

Coney
Graysby
Speckled Hind
Marbled Grouper
Misty Grouper
Snowy Grouper
Yellowedge Grouper

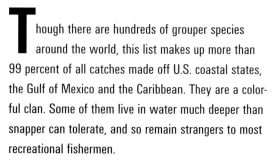

Though there are hundreds of grouper species around the world, this list makes up more than 99 percent of all catches made off U.S. coastal states, the Gulf of Mexico and the Caribbean. They are a colorful clan. Some of them live in water much deeper than snapper can tolerate, and so remain strangers to most recreational fishermen.

All are good or great on the table, though the bigger fish (goliath, black and warsaw) get a little tough with age. In addition, the black and yellowfin frequenting coral reefs off some islands have on occasion been implicated in ciguatera poisoning.

For simplicity's sake, we've grouped our groupers here according to similar characteristics. The first are the major players that make up sizeable catches in U.S. recreational fisheries. The remainder are bunched according to their common depths, with a caveat—these fish do migrate back and forth. Some have a wider range than others, too.

The second group is found mostly in fairly shallow water with an affinity for coral bottom. The third group makes up the "middle fish," often found in 200 to 400 feet around wrecks and rockpiles. The fourth group are deepwater or "deep-drop" species, often found in 500 to 1,000 feet.

Red grouper above patrols through "live bottom," made up of soft corals and sponges. At right, a trophy black grouper landed.

TOP
THREE
GROUPER

GAG

1. **GAG GROUPER**
2. **BLACK GROUPER**
3. **RED GROUPER**

America's top three grouper certainly have a huge following of bottom fishermen.

BLACK

Ever catch a really big grouper? It's enough to make your day, even when the weather isn't so perfect. These fish have a brute strength you never forget, once the line comes tight. They don't come easy, since all

RED

have a knack for plowing back into handy bottom cover, lodging themselves tight where they can't be pulled loose. At least, not without some patience and a few tricks described throughout this book. Catching big grouper off-shore takes a little more technique than just baiting up hooks with gobs of squid. Unless you're visiting from some faraway land, in which case you might catch a 40-pounder on the first try.

This fine gag was taken from an artificial reef off Jacksonville, Florida. Live pinfish did the trick.

The Grouper Family

❶ GAG GROUPER

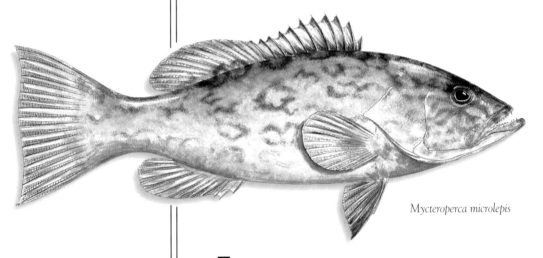

Mycteroperca microlepis

If red snapper are the queens of offshore reefs, then the gag grouper must be king. For a down and dirty fight, a fish that can pull you right out of your deck shoes, *nothing* beats a gag grouper. These fish spend the majority of their lives within inches of something they can dive into, just to keep themselves off your dinner plate. Hooking and horsing them away from cover isn't easy, either. They can be moody all day, then eat anything that passes by, but only for a half hour. Other days, they'll let a live sardine bounce off their heads. When they do feel the sting of a hook, you'd better hold on to that rod!

Many old-timers believed that gags spent their entire lives on one piece of structure. The truth is, they almost rival mahi-mahi in earning frequent swimmer miles. When biologists in South Carolina tagged some gags, they found that 22 percent of their 435 recaptures had migrated more than 150 miles. Off Jacksonville, anglers caught many of those tagged fish after a hurricane slammed the Carolinas. Apparently, hurricanes send the gags packing south for a Florida vacation. In the Gulf, similar storms send thousands of Florida gags into new waters, where they're caught from coastal piers and bridges, channel markers and new spots offshore still undiscovered by man. Tagged gags off the Suwannee River in Florida have been recovered off Texas and Vera Cruz, Mexico. So they're a widespread fish that loves to wander.

On Florida's west side where the gag is still tops,

WHEN GAGS SPAWN

Gags meet up many miles offshore in deeper water to spawn, usually from January to March. Responsible anglers tread lightly on such spawning aggregations. The problem is that all gags begin as females. If they survive about 15 years, they become males. These big "copperbellies," though fewer than females, are more aggressive and vulnerable to overfishing. It's possible to disrupt the fertilization of eggs by catching too many 20- to 50-pounders in one area. After a successful spawn, young gags move inshore. They're camouflaged and prosper on the grassflats, eating pinfish.

❶ GAG GROUPER

Gags
by Season

small fish numbering perhaps in the millions inhabit inshore grassbeds and rock patches. When they grow to eight or 10 inches, they begin easing out to slightly deeper water. But gags don't follow the rules; each year, some big

Fighting grouper all day may result in various bruises.

fish return, even to bay waters.

They're certainly the more dominant grouper on Florida's shallower reefs, especially fish of legal size. Summer may bring an influx of red grouper to shallow hard bottom, but almost all are undersized. Gags, however, of 15 pounds or so are commonly caught within sight of land, and even inside some deeper bays, especially Tampa Bay. Captain Gary Folden, who has grouper-fished along Clearwater Beach for at least 20 years, has caught gags exceeding 20 pounds in as little as 20 feet of water—within sight of passing cars and suntanned bodies. Big gags are also commonly dragged from rocks in a mere six to eight feet of water off Homosassa and Crystal River, where they hit topwater plugs!

And, the gag's name shouldn't scare people away from eating them. On the Gulf or Atlantic Coast, this is considered the best grouper of all on the table, with the possible

GAGS MIGRATE OFFSHORE WITH THE SEASONS

WINTER can slow or stop the great fall action on these fish. How much impact winter has on gags strictly depends on how many severe cold fronts pass through that area. Two factors determine the fishing: water clarity and temperature. Both dictate the moods and migrations of these fish.

After a strong cold front, the water becomes murky and colder. A mild front may have little negative effect. Gags will

bite even in mildly murky water during this time, but accurate anchoring here is a must. With reduced bottom visibility, these fish can't locate your bait unless it is close. Patiently anchoring and using a weighted chum bag on the bottom helps.

A severe cold front will shut down the grouper fishery for several days or longer. With a high barometric pressure, some captains

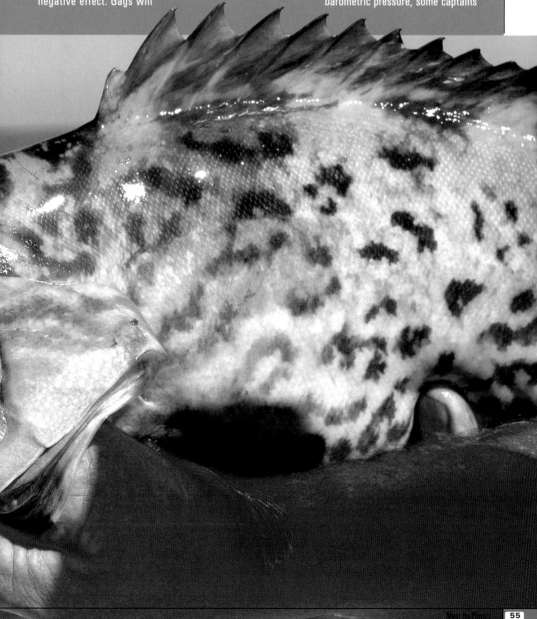

exception of scamp.

The gag is sometimes mistakenly referred in the Gulf as "black" or "gray" grouper, because they're very similar. The true black grouper is a tropical fish of the Caribbean rarely found in the U.S. except in South Florida and the Keys. Black groupers do turn up from time to time all over the Gulf of Mexico, but they're usually lone fish in deeper water that have grown large and wandered far.

This big gag attacked a live pinfish, two days after a storm passed, which had new gags roaming more common spots.

Gags by Season _{continued}

in winter refuse to go out after a cold front, until light winds return from the south. That's when the fish turn on.

A succession of cold fronts will cause the shallow areas to stay stirred up, forcing grouper to eventually migrate to deeper water, fleeing as water temperatures drop too low. Often, those close-in spots that produced great fall action become void of grouper. This commonly happens in January. However, several freezes in November (still good fishing) may bring about a very bad December on the inshore spots. The grouper pull out en masse, migrating offshore into deeper and warmer water. A severe winter with freezing temperatures reaching into Florida orange groves means that gag fishing is over for a few weeks, unless one fishes much farther offshore. Local water temps in the mid to low-50s can put grouper into near-hibernation. They tuck up in the rocks, move very little, and feed even less. Catching them is nearly impossible. When they warm slightly and begin to feed again, they'll be scratched up, caused by close contact with coral growth.

Not many anglers fish offshore in winter, but for those who do, the bite of a gag in cold weather is subtle and soft. Sometimes just a slow and steady tug is the only indication something has picked up your bait. Lift your rod tip, and it may feel like pulling your hook through Jello. It's a very soft bite.

SPRING ushers in the return of better gag fishing. As the water warms, these fish become more active, easing back inshore with the clear water. Their return to shallow reefs seems to coincide with the return of baitfish, mostly sardine and cigar minnows. Gags will even follow these pods of bait as they return inshore. That's when a livewell full of baitfish suddenly becomes a popular item. The gags are hungry, and tired of winter's meager menu. In

This angler drifting in deep water may hook more than he bargained for, if a big gag slams into his bait.

the clear waters of spring, when plankton hasn't had time to bloom yet, and floating sargassum weed is scarce, gags will chase after trolled plugs, or trolled, heavy jigs tipped with a sardine. Action can be better than autumn's bite. And, the first boats of spring have a shot at these fish before the summer crowds arrive. So, it's best to stock up on live pinfish if a few are available, and make an early trip in March if weather cooperates.

SUMMER will find gags scattered throughout their entire range, from six feet of water out to 200 feet. The shallowest water becomes perhaps too warm and makes gags somewhat lethargic. That's when many anglers make the longer runs offshore, where water temperatures on the bottom remain cool. Many anglers catch their own live baits and haul them offshore, since live baits are more easily acquired in summer.

Tropical storms and hurricanes also move these fish. After a good storm, gags will congregate around any large structure. Big ledges and sizeable wrecks give grouper the best cover from strong currents. In the Gulf, big storms have an unusual effect. Before bag limits, one could catch 80 or 100 gags in a trip, within five miles of the Destin coastline in Florida. Gags will actually head for the beach during a storm. Many gags have been caught from the Destin bridge, soon after a passing hurricane.

Summer trolling for gags can be quite slow. There are lots of baitfish schools by then.

FALL is invariably the best season to find a limit of gags. More of the bigger fish move inshore, if only for three months or less. Those long boat runs offshore become unnecessary, and there's no use wasting gas. This is when gags lose their summer malaise, often feeding recklessly during fall. They're far more aggressive in newly cooled water. This fine action continues until water temperatures dip into the mid-60s.

The ultimate time of year for Atlantic gags is when early fall northeasters are moving through, and schools of menhaden are on the beach. Wait for the wind to die down, and head offshore. Drop a live pogy down on your favorite ledge, and hold on tight. The Gulf Coast boys like the winter better, when fishing pressure is lighter, and fish congregate on some of the deeper spots.

There are a few reasons why Atlantic and especially North Florida grouper fishermen love fall weather. Not only is there a chill in the air, energizing fishermen, but the water is cooling. The fish are aware that tougher times are just around the corner. It's hard to measure what effect everyday fishing pressure has on specific spots, but each time the wind keeps anglers at the dock for a few weeks, it's a good idea to carry lots of bait on that fall trip offshore—you will need them. SB

Trophy grouper of a lifetime: This huge black grouper was caught while drift-fishing in the Florida Keys. Photo courtesy of Capt. Ralph Delph.

The Grouper Family

② BLACK GROUPER

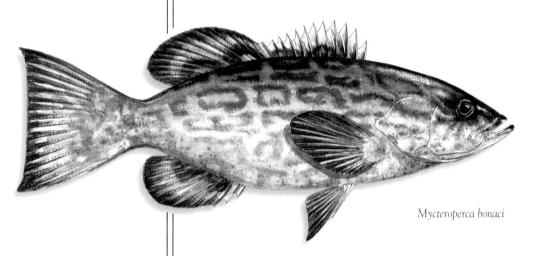

Mycteroperca bonaci

The mighty black grouper is third largest of our grouper after goliath and warsaw. Its big size (nearly 100 pounds) and ability to rise more than a hundred feet to the surface to blast a passing bait makes this the sportiest of all groupers. This is a tropical fish, relegated mostly to South Florida, The Bahamas and more southern latitudes. Big blacks, however, at times wander across the Gulf to Texas. On Florida Keys reefs and wrecks, this grouper rules the bottom; they've made an amazing comeback after legal commercial traps and bottom longlines were removed from the Atlantic coast. Recreational size and bag limits have also helped a great deal.

Years ago when Nassau grouper were abundant on Florida reefs, they were said to be the most aggressive of all grouper. Perhaps that is why the black grouper learned to feed high in the water column, to get away from unruly Nassaus on the bottom. Over time, the Nassau population collapsed in the Keys while the black has hung on, and even made a comeback. Now the black rules the reefs, until someone figures out how to reintroduce Nassaus to Florida waters.

Down in Key West, many anglers consid-

DID YOU KNOW?

> Black grouper are the top reef predator in the Florida Keys, if you discount sharks or barracuda.

> The presence of a huge male black grouper is apparently responsible for the vitality of each spawning aggregation. Dozens of female grouper will gather around one male.

> The aggressive nature of male groupers means they're often first to attack a passing bait.

> With this fish, many anglers using jigs can out-catch the livebait anglers.

er Capt. Ralph Delph to be the dean of light tackle grouper anglers, with numerous world records. He catches black grouper in as shallow as 12 feet of water out to about 260 feet, and has explored the reefs and wrecks out beyond the Dry Tortugas, which is 68 miles farther

these fish, and some of the huge grouper landed with 10- to 20-pound line are amazing, candidates for world records.

Delph uses 6- to 9-ounce jigs with no-stretch line. He's a strong proponent of curly plastic tails. He makes the jig swim up two or three feet, then lets it swim down rapidly. He never lets it go a second without tension on the lure. About 90 percent of his strikes happen on the drop. It's more like deep pulling than deep jigging.

Drift-fishing with live pinfish is the ticket.

"The point of using that much jig weight is keeping the line taut," Delph says. "You can make that lure dive to the bottom, even with tension on the line. Mono line just takes too long to signal a strike. Synthetic line makes you feel it on the drop. Jigging ballyhoo is deadly, too. As I like to say, use any color as long as it's white. Curly plastic tails that glow are best. Bait is deadly for grouper, but we can go offshore without that."

Captain Jack Carlson of Marathon, right, watches his young client from Cleveland boat a 31-pound black grouper. Not bad for a first-timer.

In December through June, many black grouper move around on some sort of west. His observations on grouper are based on a lifetime of hard-earned experience.

Delph's favorite grouper techniques fly in the face of conventional grouper wisdom, that demands heavy tackle. Like Rick Ryals, Delph feels that heavier tackle provokes these fish into getting tough, making them lunge for the nearest cover with all of their considerable power. Lighter tackle has a different effect on

migration, with the very biggest fish appearing in June over flat bottom they're not normally found on. That's when light tackle works best on them, because of less cover. When hooked they can make long runs, but they can't seem to find cover. In the rockier places they normally prefer, they're more scarce at this time.

Savvy trollers in the Keys pursue black grouper from December through February.

Black grouper of this size are easily capable of grabbing and gulping down live baits up to five pounds.

Black Grouper Spawners

DURING THE SPAWN, black grouper gather in small groups to "nest up" in one area. They don't really build a nest, but form small gatherings. The largest blacks are males, just like gags. The females congregate around a single, big male. Capt. Ralph Delph says conservation of these fish is critical off Key West, however. He's been through it several times: Clean out one of these nests, and the fish don't come back. He catches two or three from a gathering, and then will leave it alone. He says every time he caught what might be called the dominant or alpha male grouper on a spot, after that it was only a mediocre gathering of fish. Take away the big fish that draws all the spawning attention, and the females don't come around nearly as much after that. As for spawning seasons, he has found egg roe in black grouper every month during winter and spring. SB

② BLACK GROUPER

After that, trolling action slows down. But winter is prime, when there seems to be a push of these fish into shallower waters, from 15 feet on out. Fifty feet is a good, average depth in winter. Keys locals use the Mann's Stretch 30 and other big-lipped plugs to work depths from 30 to 50 feet. Some like the big-lipped MirrOlures, which dive from 12 to 15 feet.

A favorite there is the green back with silver flash, and a white belly—a very good plug. In the Stretch models, many prefer tiger or orange with a white belly. You can troll up some grouper year-round with those plugs. Sandy alleyways bordering high-relief coral ledges are prime trolling territory. With polarizing sunglasses, you can really see shallow grouper bottom on the Atlantic side of the Keys. Now and then, a black grouper surprises an angler trolling surface lures for sailfish or dolphin in much deeper water. In the dog days

Fresh ballyhoo baits attract plenty

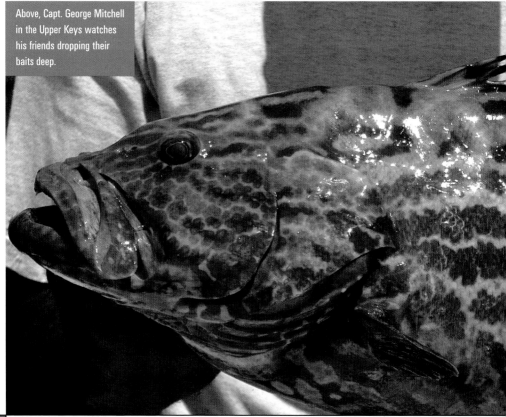

Above, Capt. George Mitchell in the Upper Keys watches his friends dropping their baits deep.

of grouper and snapper as well.

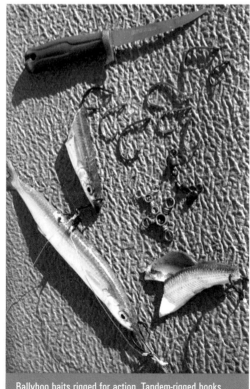

of summer, this action slows way down.

Delph does have some favorite baits for black grouper. He uses a lot of pinfish, just like grouper specialist Capt. Jack Carlson does in Marathon. (Jack has worked on a few grouper records as well, including a huge gag.) Both captains set out a couple of pinfish traps and it's an easy chore to pick them up before heading out to the reef. Ballyhoo are a favorite reef bait as well, attracting a variety of grouper and snapper. Legal-size yellowtail snapper are also great for tempting big blacks on the reefs, as are goggle-eyes. Many captains say black grouper aren't really that particular, but that a good-sized bait works best. Delph says a 2- or 3-pound yellowtail, alive, is a very fine bait. Hook it through the back and drop it down in 70 to 100 feet, and watch what happens. That's why reef captains carry a big stick, even while yellowtail fishing. A black grouper may appear and begin grabbing hooked fish, and the heavy rod is reserved for them.

There doesn't seem an appreciable difference in eating quality between blacks of 40 to 50 pounds and a 20-pounder. Delph personally won't eat grouper too big. He says a 40-pound grouper is 20 years old; if you catch a 40-pounder, chances are you'll catch a 20-pounder the same day. It's better to eat the smaller one and release the bigger fish. Big female grouper carry more eggs, while the big, aggressive males so critical for spawning aggregations are definitely in shorter supply. They're almost like trophy deer; they represent the biggest and strongest in the gene pool.

Ballyhoo baits rigged for action. Tandem-rigged hooks, butterflied and chunked baits, favorite hooks.

Here's the vital bottom fish for Tampa-St.Petersburg grouper diggers, the red grouper.

The Grouper Family

❸ RED GROUPER

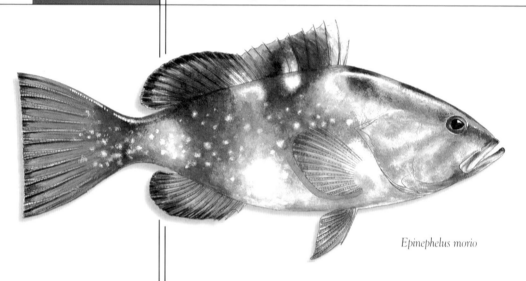

Epinephelus morio

Though not really red, this grouper is normally a dark rust color—when it isn't trying to camouflage itself over white sand. The red grouper is a little more sedentary than his cousins, and doesn't get around as much, preferring to wait by a handy hole or ledge for something tasty to pass by. They do migrate some and forage actively when the tide is running. Numerous in their home waters off Southwest Florida, they're none too picky about what they eat. That makes them a favorite with bottom fishermen, including the partyboat crowd. That's where millions of pounds of reds have been landed each year, from hundreds of square miles of what they call "live bottom" off that coast.

To target keeper-sized red grouper, a fish that may average five pounds, most anglers anchor. Others drift, because they know reds are famous for scattering across acres of live, mostly flat rock bottom that supports sponges, sea fans and other marine growth. This is a fine-tasting grouper, though some say not as good as the gag, which inhabits the very same waters.

Red grouper take their time growing to a legal length, while their girth expands instead. After a great year class of young reds begins to mature offshore, it's possible to catch 50 of these fish on a good day, with

DID YOU KNOW?

> Red grouper favor low-profile reefs called "live bottom," made up of various soft corals.

> A master of camouflage, reds are almost invisible until they suddenly dart from cover.

> Nicknamed "garbagemouth" by some anglers, the red isn't nearly as finicky an eater as some fish. And with a big mouth, they can wrap up almost anything that passes by.

> Not as smart as the gag grouper, the red doesn't fare well when spearfishermen invade his turf.

lots of bruising action, but with no keepers for the fishbox. They may be solid fish, but not quite long enough to keep. Catch too many short reds, and you may run out of bait offshore before finding some keeper fish. Veteran anglers bring lots of frozen, fresh and live bait, and they don't mind filleting fresh grunts or sand perch to sweeten the hooks. For this kind of fishing, keep a cutting board handy on the boat.

On the shallower Florida Gulf Coast, from St. Marks (near Tallahassee) on south, reaching red grouper bottom often means traveling a long way offshore. These fish love the 100-foot depths, which can be a prohibitive run for many boats on that coast. They're also shy of cold weather, and migrate—even disappear—when harsh weather drops water temperatures. Other

Reds by Season

Because red grouper in many areas are seasonal, we've listed a guide to their availability, courtesy of Capt. Gary Folden.

Red grouper that aren't quite legal can easily be scooped out with a landing net, and released.

grouper species don't seem to mind chilly weather as much, but a week of cold weather will often evict red grouper from a shallow spot in December that offered fast action in November.

Bigger, solitary reds are found in deeper water, down to 300 feet. At those depths cold weather doesn't penetrate, so it's a year-round

Without a doubt, SUMMER is the best time of year to find red grouper on the west coast. The weather here is more dependable for runs offshore to deep water, where the larger reds are found. Any show of fish on the fishfinder on hard bottom areas in 80 to 150 feet is worth stopping and checking for reds. Don't be surprised if gags or mangrove snapper get into the fray.

The FALL season can still be (and usually is) hot for red grouper. Depending on water temperatures, reds will remain on their summer haunts. This fishery is often ignored in the fall, due to an influx of gags into nearshore waters. In fact, reds will bite fast and hard on chilly November days, when the bottom temperature hasn't had time to drop yet.

WINTER is a difficult time to catch red grouper. The fishery remains more active in more southerly regions of the Florida Gulf. Winter landings of red grouper from Sanibel Island to Marco Island are not uncommon. The problem is that the cold fronts so prevalent at this time of year can make the long runs offshore very rough and undesirable.

SPRING is the start of the red grouper fishing for most of the west coast. April and May are the peak spawning months, and mark the beginning of better fishing in summer weather. SB

Juicy reef offerings for red grouper and others: the heavy jig tipped with something sweet (fresh baitfish). Below, fresh ballyhoo bait rigged with tandem stinger hook.

fishery. Most anglers never actually fish that deep for them, with exceptions. One fisherman from Crystal River liked to troll almost 200 feet down with cable gear and planers. He reports catching red grouper up to 30 pounds with that method. His trolling covered a wide expanse of bottom that had probably never been fished before. Also in that deeper water, remote controlled cameras have documented red grouper sitting in huge depressions in the sand bottom that were up to 20 feet in diameter. The holes closely resembled huge nests, like a freshwater bass would make. It's unknown how these big holes were created in the Gulf.

Drift fishing is a great way to locate and catch red grouper. Conditions must be right for this to happen, however. The angler must be over hard bottom and the wind and current gentle enough for bait and lead to reach bottom easily. If a red grouper is hooked, make a note of the location using a GPS, or throw a marker jug and re-drift the area. Some of the best red grouper action is found where sandbars roll down into hardbottom areas. Look for baitfish over the sandbar, or suspended over the rocks. This is a prime setup for catching a limit of reds.

Large jigs are a great alternative here, to the standard sinker and hook rigs. Jigs work best when drifting, bouncing off bottom every minute or so. Those with large plastic tails work great, but tipping the jig with a small piece of squid or fish is a meal ticket. Some

Jigs with large plastic tails work great, but tipping the jig with a small

Above, rod and reel with bottom rig for digging grouper from rough bottom. Below, a good variety of frozen bait for tempting bottom fish.

anglers take a whole cigar minnow or Spanish sardine and nose-hook it directly to a bare jig.

Keep in mind that red grouper will eat any natural bait good enough for gags. One difference is that the red is not nearly as picky as the gag. Since they will devour just about anything that passes by, they've no doubt earned some ungenerous nicknames over the years.

Down in the Keys and the southeastern coastline of Florida, keeper red grouper live within sight of land, where the depths drop off fast. Their numbers have dwindled where fishing pressure is high, however. The vast expanse of Gulf off Southwest Florida, stretching almost 100 miles out, offers much more potential.

piece of squid or fish is a meal ticket.

CORAL GROUPERS

These include the small hinds and coneys that are all beautiful, though they're the smallest of the clan. Nassau, tigers and yellowmouth are larger. All of them, however, can be found in fairly shallow water over a rich, coral bottom.

SCAMP

Here is the tastiest grouper of all. The secret among old-timers, before scamp were identified by the public, was to always keep scamp for themselves, while selling their snapper and other fish. You simply *don't* give a scamp away. How to tell the difference? The scamp has a "broom" tail, very ragged looking compared to other groupers.

While found in the northern Gulf, especially

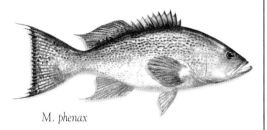

M. *phenax*

around the 30-fathom rocks offshore, the scamp is also common along the Atlantic coast from Fort Pierce, Florida up into Georgia.

There, they can actually be taken while trolling diving plugs just off the beach, over shallow reefs in about 20 feet of water. Farther north they remain a prize in deeper water, hitting fresh cut bait. In Fernandina, one may see a charterboat just returned from 40 miles offshore, unloading a dozen or more of these beauties in a single day, with perhaps a couple of gags mixed in, and a load of vermilion snapper.

As a sidenote, these same fish have been observed by scuba divers at the deep oil rigs in the Gulf, in 900 feet of water. The scamps were hovering at the 100-foot level inside the structure, seemed almost tame, and averaged at least 15 pounds.

So, a very versatile fish. Best way to target them? Anchor on the 30-fathom rocks offshore, and use circle hooks with fresh cut bait.

GOLIATH (formerly jewfish)

Legendary stories abound of goliath grouper, formerly known as the "jewfish." Any inshore, indeed, shallow-water fish that grows to 800 pounds is bound to cause conflict when in close proximity with fishermen and scuba divers. And these guys are brutes. Fully grown goliaths have been described on various occasions as having the same dimensions as a Volkswagen Beetle.

Goliaths prefer shelter, living inside sunken shipwrecks, springs, concrete culverts used for artificial reefs, and holes around jetties and bridges. Even undercut banks beneath mangrove forests.

Federally protected since 1990, these fish have staged a comeback, with anglers on

Spawning aggregation of huge goliath grouper in the Florida Keys. Average weight per fish: 300 pounds. Photo courtesy of Don DeMaria.

Florida's west coast petitioning to have goliaths opened for retention. In some areas like Crystal River, goliaths actively stalk hooked fish, grabbing grouper, snapper and other bottomfish before they can be safely landed. As a result, goliaths are a great fish for hook and release fishing—big, strong, and since they're caught in shallow water, not prone to damage from inflated air bladders. For many anglers, goliaths often are the biggest fish they are likely to catch.

E. itajara

To target goliaths, use a stout rod with at least 80-pound line, a heavier mono leader, a non-stainless steel hook, and a big bait. Salty captains swear that a live jack crevalle of 3-4 pounds is best.

However, the old-timers who caught and sold "jewfish" as they were known back then, often preferred a live stingray about the size of a dinner plate, with the poisonous barb removed.

When they were legal to keep, smaller jewfish were certainly better on the table than the tough old fish of 300 pounds and more. Bigger specimens have many thin layers of fat inside the fillets.

CORAL GROUPERS

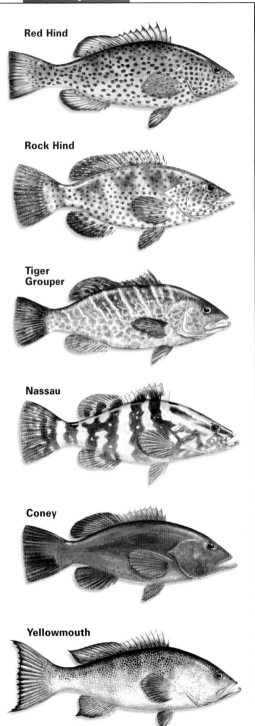

Red Hind

Rock Hind

Tiger Grouper

Nassau

Coney

Yellowmouth

RED HIND *E. guttatus*

Quite common in The Bahamas, making up a large part of the catch over coral reefs. They must be very prolific. They'll attack a frozen bait almost their size.

Covered in red spots, with a pinkish background. In The Bahamas, anchor up in 40 feet of water over rocky bottom, day or night, and it's rather easy to catch a few red hinds for the skillet. Quite good on the table. Hinds have a small tail, so don't expect much of a fight.

ROCK HIND *E. adscensionis*

This is a smallish grouper, topping out at five pounds or so. Though widely dispersed around the Caribbean, South Atlantic and Gulf of Mexico, one never seems to see more than a few of these fish on a good day. And the majority average two pounds at best.

Most rock hinds, nicknamed "calico" grouper, are caught incidentally while bottom fishing in the Gulf, on the rocks and reefs in perhaps 40 to 100 feet of water.

They're certainly not picky, and will bite any fresh chunk of cut bait.

Other rock hinds are taken in The Bahamas over coral bottom, caught alongside more numerous red hinds. In the western Gulf, rockies prowl up and down the coral-covered legs of oil rigs, sometimes within 10 feet of the surface, and will pounce on small jigs tipped with fresh bait, when worked through the structure. Or bounced over rocky patches, for that matter.

TIGER GROUPER *M. tigris*

A fine figure of a grouper, they seem to entirely favor coral bottom, and they can be seen prowling around in broad daylight. They're a classic-looking grouper if one exists, with a big head and teeth, and the square tail required for frequent jaunts. This is a dark, almost olive-green fish, with irregular bars and lots of white speckles. They're probably a terror for small fish, squid, shrimp or crabs. Grows to at least 8 pounds.

NASSAU GROUPER *E. striatus*

This is the classic, big grouper often pictured on the cover of so many dive magazines. A master of camouflage, they're also a top predator on the reef, growing up to 55 pounds.

Nassaus suffered severe setbacks in some parts of the Caribbean, and are now protected from harvest in U.S. waters. Rare in the entire Gulf of Mexico, the only Nassaus caught near Florida are in the Keys, over coral or deeper rock bottom. It's a shame the Nassau, formerly the dominant bottom predator there ahead of black grouper, is now in dire straits. But they're vulnerable to trapping, and they gather in (formerly) huge spawning aggregations each winter, where they can be caught just before spawning. Nominated as an endangered species in Florida, someone should be transplanting new stock from The Bahamas to the Lower Florida Keys.

CONEY *E. fulvus*

Coneys are another of the small, colorful groupers best photographed when they're peeking out of some coral hideyhole. This is another lurker that prefers to wait in ambush until something tasty is within short range. Said to have two distinct spots at the tip of the lower jaw. This is just another small bonus grouper, taken while fishing over coral bottom.

Classy rock hind grouper only grows to about 3 pounds.

YELLOWMOUTH GROUPER
M. interstitialis

Another handsome grouper, brown with darker spots, yellow jaws and a yellow tail tip. They're well-equipped for cruising around the reef, with the square tail. Sometimes mistaken for scamp, small yellowmouth often frequent the same waters and may actually outnumber scamp populations in the western Gulf of Mexico.

They're quick to pounce on passing jigs, and in fact seem to have the same feeding habits as scamp. Their tail, however, does not become ragged with the larger individuals, as with the scamp. With a Florida record of 28 pounds, this is a significant fish.

Yellowmouth grouper moves among the live coral, hunting for dinner.

MIDDLE GROUPERS

The grouper in this section lurk in the mid-bottoms from 180 to 400 feet, often a good ways beyond the coast or reefs, but still inshore of the deeper waters of 500 to 1,000 feet that constitute "deep-drop" fishing. Some of these species move back and forth when it suits them, and can't be pinned to a single depth of bottom. Warsaw are the most notorious depth changers, traveling from 1,000-foot depths in summer or fall to only 90 feet in early spring, to spawn.

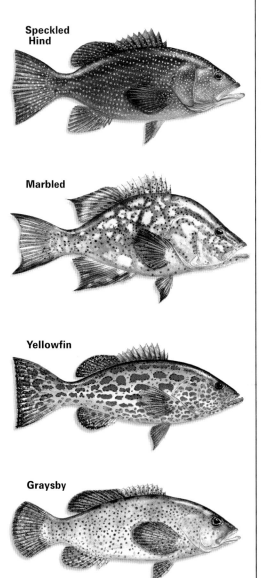

Speckled Hind

Marbled

Yellowfin

Graysby

SPECKLED HIND
E. drummondhayi

Perhaps the most interesting is the beautiful speckled hind, often called "Kitty Mitchell." How did a grouper get a human's name? Legend has it that Kitty Mitchell was a lovely redheaded babe with freckles, who was highly popular with many of the first Gulf snapper fishermen, probably out of Pensacola, where most of the fleet was based. The nickname has stuck for more than a century. Common at around five pounds, the Kitty Mitchell's world record is said to be 64 pounds. Best depths are 150 to 300 feet. Most are caught by accident. Populations are thought to be low, so only one of these fish is allowed on a boat each day.

MARBLED GROUPER *E. inermis*

This grouper is rather different from the others, shaped more like a heavy-bodied tripletail than the rest of the clan. Most marbled groupers appear to average about 15 pounds. They can change colors, but often are a mix of red with white splotches.

Somewhat rare, these fish are taken around the deeper reefs in 200 to 400 feet. A small colony was discovered by submersible in the western Gulf around the isolated Flower Gardens reef. They can also be found around the deepwater drilling platforms that sit even in 900 feet, with "marbles" observed hanging around the pilings at a depth of 150 feet.

One may surmise these same fish have hangouts along the 30-fathom dropoffs off Port St. Joe, Florida, and perhaps out beyond the Middle Grounds as well.

Not really targeted, they're an unexpected, incidental catch while bottom fishing with cut bait. Quite good on the table, however.

YELLOWFIN GROUPER *M. venenosa*

Here is a classy grouper, better-dressed than most of his clan. The yellowfin (of course) sports yellow fins, but with a pinkish belly. The body may be olive in color, other times a dark, reddish hue. Reaching 30 pounds and almost 4 feet, the yellowfin competes with black grouper for its prey on coral reefs, especially in The Bahamas. Though caught on shallower coral reefs, where they're seen even by snorkel divers, one may find a good concentration of bigger yellowfins on some deepwater rock in 200 to 400 feet.

During spring, along with black grouper, they prowl the coral dropoffs and will slam into trolled, diving plugs in The Bahamas.

They're also found across the Gulf of Mexico, notably on the remote, 30-fathom rocks that receive less fishing pressure. The hot bite on many of these deeper rocks is just after dark, until perhaps 10:30 p.m. That is when the Texas state record was caught by one angler, after his crew had fallen asleep. The fish weighed 31 pounds, and struck half of a blue runner fished on bottom.

The yellowfin is seldom targeted in U.S. waters, though popular in The Bahamas. Implicated in some cases of ciguatera poisoning.

GRAYSBY *C. cruentatus*

Despite the name, graysby is a beautiful, red-spotted fish that hangs out around the 30-fathom rocks. His tail section is less developed than the bigger reef groupers. This would indicate the graysby doesn't get around much, but hides in holes, dashing out to grab passing prey. He's like one of the small hind groupers found on the reefs, only bigger, and has a black spot near the dorsal fin that helps aid in identification. Grows to almost 15 pounds.

Not really targeted, this is just one more surprise of a grouper that can be caught when bottom fishing on the 30-fathom rocks. Like all of these mid-depth groupers, they're quite good on the table.

Above, yellowfin grouper caught in The Bahamas. Middle, rare marbled grouper lurks at 155 feet. Bottom, the rare speckled hind, often called "Kitty Mitchell."

DEEP GROUPERS

These are the "deep-drop" groupers, lurking in depths from 500 to 1,000 feet. Most specimens caught from deep water inflate so badly, it's difficult to imagine what they look like when alive. Few people have ever watched a deepwater grouper while on the bottom, unless they sat in a deepsea submersible. All four of these grouper are good to eat, with white, flaky meat. Catching a 20- to 50-pounder on a deep drop is certainly worth the effort of bringing these fish up.

When finally cranked up, these fish become helpless and increasingly more buoyant. When hooked at 900 feet for instance, the gas inside them expands 27 times on the way up, a fatal case of the "bends." If the hook slips out at the surface, these fish almost always float.

Snowy

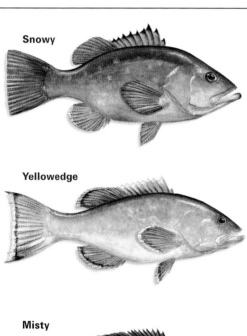

Yellowedge

Misty

Warsaw

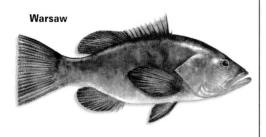

SNOWY GROUPER *E. niveatus*

Big snowy grouper somewhat resemble warsaw, in that they are fairly dark and colorless. Though similar, the snowy has scattered, large white spots, and a much smaller dorsal fin than the warsaw. Snowies commonly grow to 50 pounds in remote areas that see little fishing pressure, often in depths of about 900 feet. Best bait for this grouper is a fresh fillet of blue runner. Small snowies are sometimes caught inshore, and when acclimated to shallow water, make an attractive member of large, saltwater aquariums. However, they're very territorial and will kill larger fish, even each other when paired up.

YELLOWEDGE GROUPER
E. flavolimbatus

These guys carry white spots as well, but the defining I.D. factor here is a ridge of yellow color on the dorsal fin. Available in commercial numbers in the Gulf, they've been caught in considerable quantity in previous years by bottom longliners. This fish commonly grows to slightly over 30 pounds. Use chunks of cut bait or small, whole fish.

MISTY GROUPER *E. mystacinus*

With a record misty grouper of slightly over 200 pounds, this is another major fish from deep water. Juvenile misties are sometimes caught on the 30-fathom rocks. Bigger specimens may venture beyond the 1,000-foot depths. Scattered all over the western Atlantic and Gulf, this is said to be the only grouper in the Caribbean with a pattern of regular, dark bars on its sides. This is a fairly rare, solitary fish. Catching two on the same day would be an occasion indeed.

WARSAW GROUPER *E. nigritus*

A hulking brute that can just exceed 300 pounds, warsaw have gained more of a reputation in the Gulf of Mexico than along the Atlantic coast, even though they're widespread. Each spring, bigger warsaw venture inshore to spawn in waters where the partyboat fleet anchors in depths of 90 to 200 feet, and that is when most are caught. Where these fish are during the remainder of the year is a mystery, but they're sometimes caught as deep as 1,200 feet by the few anglers who drift and make deep drops. Oil company crews working on the deepwater oil rigs in the western Gulf, on the edge of the continental shelf in about 900 feet of water, caught plenty of big warsaw when it was legal to do so. (Their favorite bait was a live, two-pound blue runner.)

Because of their slow growth and their constantly losing ground to fishing pressure, the warsaw bag limit is limited to one per boat. They've become far more scarce than a few years ago, when some partyboat trips in February and March specifically targeted them, with each angler using a stout handline. Prior to that they were a pest on the red snapper banks, stealing fish off the hooks, forcing some of the old commercial snapper boats to pull

This small warsaw grouper hit a jig in 70 feet. Above, another warsaw skulks at sunken tugboat in 95 feet.

anchor and relocate.

To target warsaw grouper, try using live vermilion snapper, which seem to frequent the same (relatively inshore) depths. Big warsaw are a little tough on the table, and for that reason, and the fact that stocks are stressed, they should probably be avoided or released. SB

CHAPTER 2

Other Players

The oceans offer a great variety of fish, especially on the bottom. Nobody is better acquainted with variety than snapper and grouper fishermen, who become well-used to a colorful assortment of fish landing on deck. Many of these fish are common acquaintances, welcome back home and good on the fork, as they say. Others are commonly tossed back or used for cutbait. Popular bottom species, of which there are a dozen or more in good numbers, are normally kept for the kitchen. We've listed a few of them here that are widespread and nearly as tasty as snapper or grouper. Keep in mind that the list can change from one generation to another, as one popular species declines and another takes it place.

Each species makes for good sport when matched against the right tackle.

Above, amberjack prowl for dinner. Below, red porgy found in Florida waters.

The Other Guys Earn Respect

There are lots of fish in the sea, and even the saltiest captain never quite knows what surprise may show up on deck. Florida fishermen may catch any of a hundred species of saltwater fish, but there are other secondary players frequently caught by those seeking snapper and grouper. These fish make up a significant percentage of daily offshore catches and, while considered secondary, remain a welcome catch that can be taken home. Each species makes for good sport when matched with the right tackle. And they're all quite good to eat.

GRAY TRIGGERFISH

These are the cat burglars of saltwater fish. They can steal bait from a hook without the slightest nibble. For many years, they were scorned by bottom fishermen. That is, until someone finally tried cooking a few. They actually have less red meat than a snapper and they're very good on the fork.

This is an opportunistic fish, sometimes hovering at mid-depths, that will chase after baits as they're lowered to the bottom. In some parts of the Gulf of Mexico, triggerfish are so thick, some of the wrecks and rocks can't be fished during daylight hours. Schools of triggers swarm the depths in summer, and they can stop a 16-ounce lead weight that has several baits attached. Getting your hooks "shined" is a common problem in triggerfish waters. It seems that their chisel-like teeth will scratch the hooks shiny. The trick to countering this problem is to fish the same spot at night, when snapper prowl and all triggerfish sleep.

A commercial market was developed for triggerfish in the early 1990s, and coupled with the realization they were good to eat, the average size of gray triggerfish has dropped. Maximum size is about 10 pounds, and triggers of that weight are normally caught in excess of 80 feet of water.

To target triggers, use a very small but strong hook, perhaps a number 4. They'll bite on virtually all baits, but use a tough little chunk of fresh bait with the skin attached, if you want a good chance at catching one. Frozen bait that becomes soft and mushy is a very poor choice here. For a fight, try lighter spinning tackle.

Cleaning triggers is a bit of a chore, and they can dull a fillet knife with

Eight-pound gray triggerfish caught in 900 feet at Gulf oil rig.

their skin, which is thicker than shark skin. Holding a trigger by the tail, slice off the upper and lower caudal fins. Cut a ring around the tail, and then peel the skin forward toward the head. That exposes the fillet, which can be

Gray triggerfish are masters at stealing bait.

sliced out. These fish have a large head, so it takes a trigger of two or three pounds to earn respectable fillets. The smaller fish should be released.

WHITE GRUNTS

These fish have always been the bread-and-butter bottom fish off Florida's Gulf Coast. When currents are slow and snapper and grouper refuse to bite, it is white grunts that provide, very often preventing some folks from making a "water haul."

The white grunt may be one of the last plentiful fish species to get along without bag limits. Folks with a hunger for their own fish can sack them up the old-fashioned way, often filling boxes and coolers. Though they live for about 12 years, white grunts do not grow at the same rate; two hefty, 14-inch fish may be at least five years apart in age. They're prolific spawners and they scatter across the live bottom for acres and miles, dispersing very well. Or, they may bunch up around a rockpile, where they can be swiftly harvested. Old salts always say that if you're catching lots of grunts

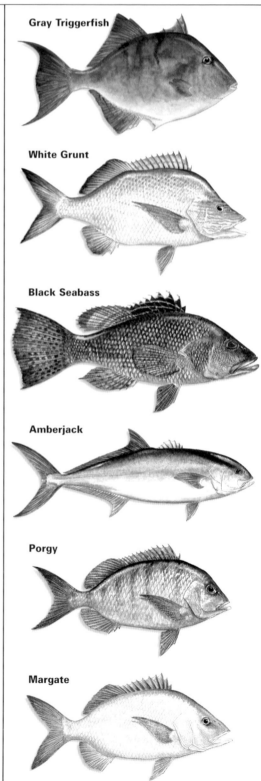

Gray Triggerfish

White Grunt

Black Seabass

Amberjack

Porgy

Margate

at a spot, very likely there are gag grouper lurking nearby. The two species function together, and grouper prey on the grunts. (The same co-mingling is more rare with seabass.)

Never a discerning fellow, the white grunt

Male seabass develop a hump on their heads. White grunts, top, are abundant and tasty.

will bite scraps of almost anything on a small hook. Despite lots of fishing pressure, grunts show up most often on Gulf headboats, where hundreds of pounds may be caught on a typical day. Without this one species, some of the headboats simply couldn't stay in business.

These fish have a place in folklore, by virtue of the fact that "grits and grunts" was a classic Florida breakfast for many years. Other species of grunts, especially down in the Keys, con-

tributed to this reputation. It originated during the hard years of the 1930s, when many folks were poor and grunts provided easy to catch, fresh seafood.

White grunts can be caught on heavier tackle, but to provide some sport, trying using spinning tackle with 10-pound line. If the current is slow, a bucktail jig of 3/8 ounce or so will easily reach prime grunt bottom in 25 to 40 feet. Tip the hook with a small piece of squid or cut bait. A good-sized grunt will bend a spinning rod into the water, putting up a much better fight than neighboring seabass.

When being filleted, grunts are spiky and somewhat bony, with the meat thin and not as delicate or white as a seabass. The meat has a slightly fishy taste, but folks who don't want their fish tasting like chicken soon acquire a real taste for it.

BLACK SEABASS

These guys are about as subtle as a Brazilian piranha, though without the sharp teeth, when confronted with a passing jig or chunk of cut bait. They rush up and gulp it down and worry about the consequences later. Many actually swallow the hook, and a pair of needlenose pliers is invaluable here. They're famous for attacking baits as large as themselves, even bashing 12-inch trolling plugs pulled a dozen feet above bottom. For a 10-inch fish, that's ambition. When drifting the boat quietly in 25 feet of water, one can hook keeper seabass and have five to seven or more excited fish follow it to the surface, where they're easy targets for more jigs. These fish are so greedy or excitable, one may catch two seabass on the same single J-hook. They will also grab a 2-

ounce bank sinker in early spring and hold on like a bulldog, until they're finally shaken free, landing on deck and soon after, into a very hot frying pan.

Somewhat territorial, seabass spread out across the live bottom patches. They hole up around tiny ledges, darting out at passing prey. Anglers almost certainly hook more seabass, and bigger ones, by drift-fishing over live bottom and rock patches.

This is another fish that is best caught with light tackle. Spin gear in the 8- to 10-pound class is best, with a short, mono leader of 20 to 40 pounds. They're certainly not leader shy. Wormtails or bucktail jigs are more sporty, too, and they can be tipped with a small piece of squid to enhance the bite.

On the cleaning table, seabass fillets are rather small, but the meat is delicate and snow white. It's fairly easy to catch a hundred seabass when the water is clear enough to visually drift over numerous patches of dark bottom between sand patches, in Florida's Big Bend on the Gulf. Cull the catch down to about 40 keeper fish in the 11- to 13-inch range, and you've got 80 fillets that will provide two separate fish fries back at home. Undersized seabass (below 10 inches) are easily released, provided they don't swallow the hook too deeply.

These guys seldom grow over about 13 inches on the Gulf side of Florida and the reason, according to marine biologists, is a parasite that locks a seabass' jaw open when it grows to that size. The result is starvation. On the Atlantic side, the very same species of seabass grows to three pounds and more.

Amberjack will even chase after trolled plugs near sunken shipwrecks.

AMBERJACK

AJs are the guardians of wrecks and deeper reefs, ready to pull the rod from a careless angler's hands. These guys are tough! And they grow to about 140 pounds, though the majority of anglers wouldn't care to try an AJ of this size, if they know what's good for them.

Undersized amberjacks provide plenty of good sport, when they can be caught in open water. For instance, those Gulf sheepshead spawning in March offshore in 20 feet of water often have schools of three-pound amberjack milling around them. The live shrimp meant for sheepshead is snapped up by these AJs, and that makes for a brisk fight on spin gear.

Anglers targeting grouper and snapper often don't mind landing a keeper AJ or two, but some spots are too well-guarded. The AJs hovering at mid-depth on down to the bottom can intercept all live bait sent their way. They're very quick and watchful. Desperate anglers have resorted to placing their bait inside a brown paper bag, sending it deep, hoping it will disintegrate on bottom, right in front of a choice grouper. However, the U.S. Coast Guard frowns on dumping paper waste overboard, and the practice isn't recommended.

Around structure, the AJ will bulldog with a hook right into cover, making things difficult for the angler. Choice, expensive bucktail jigs are lost in this manner. To target keeper AJs, try bucktail jigs from two to four ounces. Allow the jig to hit bottom, and then work it back as fast and erratically as possible to mid-depth, before dropping back down. A long rod with an upward sweep is best here, perhaps eight feet long. Either a lever drag or levelwind reel is best for this work, a strong reel with at least 40-pound mono. No leader is necessary, as these fish have no real teeth.

On the table, AJs are good enough for a neighborhood fish fry. Save the grouper and snapper for yourself, and feed the neighbors chunks of AJ fried in beer batter. AJs caught from Florida Keys reefs seem to have far more (harmless) parasites in their fillets, and many anglers there refrain from keeping their fish for this reason.

PORGY

There are six species of porgy that offshore anglers in Florida run into from time to time. Related to sheepshead and pinfish, all six porgies are good to eat. They don't carry the prestige of snapper and grouper, but their fillets, when cut into fingers, taste

Big saucereye porgy caught near the Middle Grounds in 180 feet of water.

PORGY SPECIES

>The aforementioned red porgy has thick fillets for its size, and is rumored to grow up to 20 pounds in much deeper water.

>The grass porgy, which lives up to its name out to depths of 20 feet or so, only grows to one pound.

>The world record jolthead porgy is 23 pounds, and it doesn't venture that deep. Bigger specimens are found around snapper rocks offshore.

>The knobbed porgy is more colorful, with red and purple. Fairly common up to about four pounds.

>The saucereye porgy is silvery with blue streaks and it inhabits the snapper banks. Said to reach about eight pounds.

>The whitebone porgy is also silvery with dark blotches, again growing to four pounds.

very similar around a frying pan.

Bigger porgies live in deeper water. Anglers hunting gag grouper in only 30 or 40 feet see occasional porgies, usually too small to keep. Make a serious trip offshore out to 100 feet or more, however, and porgies suddenly become a viable target.

When the grouper bite is slow, one can often find steady action on porgies by rigging three small hooks on short drops, with a 12-ounce bank sinker. The big lead speeds the little baited squid chunks to the bottom, and little time is wasted. Reeling up strong, slab-sided red porgies is a good way to ensure fresh fish on the table. It pays to carry a small box of strong but small hooks in size 1 or 2, with the hooks thick enough to resist breaking.

On partyboat trips to Florida's Middle Grounds, it's easy work cranking up several porgy at a time, while most other anglers are waiting patiently for the grouper bite to turn on. These grouper may or may not bite, but the porgies always seem to oblige in those rocky bottom environs.

MARGATE

The "white margate" is a member of the grunt family, but they grow to at least 15 pounds, and fight as hard as any snapper. This fish is shaped very much like the common (though much smaller) white grunt, from the west coast of Florida. So, they're a legitimate bonus fish when bottom fishing on the reefs, in this era of tight bag limits for snapper and grouper. Rather widespread, margates are sometimes referred to as "white snapper" because of their pale color. On the Bahama Banks they can be found in only 12 feet of water, hanging

around sunken wrecks. This is more of a tropical fish, found in South Florida and latitudes south of there. In the Dry Tortugas, big specimens are caught around the wrecks and ledges in depths down to 100 feet. At deeper wrecks in 300 feet, *schools* of big margates have been observed by divers.

Schools of 15-pound margates hang around Keys wrecks, in 300 feet.

The darker black margate more resembles a member of the drum family with its deeper body. It grows to at least 12 pounds, providing a good fight. Another shallow-water fish, this margate has been caught around rocky patches near the surf itself, including man-made structures. It's another good fish on the table. SB

CHAPTER 3

Fishing Hard Bottom and Shallow Reefs

Loading up and heading offshore with snapper and grouper in mind is a prime source of entertainment for many saltwater fishermen, in coastal states where an abundance of shallow rocks and reefs can be found in less than 80 feet of water. In most cases, anglers are searching for countless low-relief rocks and ledges, that provide a firm base for growing coral and sponges, often called "live bottom." Some of these spots may be small, but they provide habitat for big snapper and grouper, among other fish. With today's advances in marine electronics, finding such spots and fishing them effectively has evolved into an entire industry.

Young anglers admire a yellowtail snapper caught from a Florida reef.

Shallow Water Havens for Fish and Anglers

Suitable shallow bottom for snapper and grouper fishing surrounds the entire state of Florida. In the Atlantic, a narrow band of good bottom extends seaward along the southern half of Florida. Here, relic coral reefs parallel the coastline from Miami

Florida's Gulf Coast is indeed shallow, and bottomfish love it.

Shallow reefs and wrecks offer shelter and food to most bottom fish in 80 feet of water or less.

through Fort Pierce. The Florida Keys of course offer vibrant living coral reefs, of the barrier and "patch reef" varieties. Off St. Augustine and Jacksonville, the shelf widens out to 50 or more miles offshore. However, the home port for the most extensive, continental shelf fishery in the United States is actually

the west coast of Florida. The very gradual, sloping bottom offshore makes for thousands of square miles of suitable Gulf bottom for both grouper and snapper. This West Florida Shelf, as it's called, extends seaward for over 100 miles. That's a lot of fishing area. The Florida Keys may be beautiful with clear water, but it's still rather narrow when compared with the Gulf side of the state.

Florida's western Gulf (not the northern Panhandle) is indeed shallow, and bottom fish love it. From Cape Sable (the southwestern tip of the Everglades) north to Marco Island, at 10 miles offshore, an angler will find himself in about 15 feet of water. From there to Sanibel Island averages 40 feet. Farther north from Boca Grande to Tarpon Springs, the average depth is only slightly deeper. From Tarpon Springs to the Saint Marks River (where the Panhandle begins), the slope becomes even more gradual—boaters 10 miles out might only find themselves in 12 to 20 feet of water! As you move west from the Saint Marks River, the water gets somewhat deeper; between Lighthouse Point and Cape San Blas to the west, the depth at 10 miles out would again approach 60 feet.

East Coasters poke fun at the gradual, sloping Gulf, but that's the exact reason grouper and snapper find it so attractive. The bottom is mostly sand, but scattered throughout and stretching for acres are various forms of exposed limestone where coral can attach and grow. This is also home to America's big sponge beds, which provide living habitat for many fish.

These areas are critical for bottom fish, and the abundance and diversity of life is truly amazing: Flounder lie in wait along the sandy edges; red and mangrove snappers mix in among the rocks; red grouper peer out from their hiding holes or sit out in the open, camouflaged; gag grouper patrol everywhere, looking for meals, sometimes high above the structure; and schools of baitfish wander among the soft corals. Marauding mackerel, both Spanish and kings, also roam above this complex city of life.

Any angler who indulges in bottom fishing will soon learn he has more in common with hunters than with anglers who spend their time trolling. While structure is vital to both trolling and bottom fishing, you've got to be right on target to catch red snapper. Off Jacksonville, for instance, if you're trolling for kingfish within 100 yards of a good piece of structure, that's often close enough for great action. For snapper, you'd better be a lot closer than that, though they do move around better than grouper. With grouper, if you miss the spot by much more than 30 feet, you might as well be fishing in your bathtub.

If you chase bottom fish long enough, you're going to find a few honey holes that haven't been fished, and chances are good the snapper and grouper there will be huge. Truly big red snapper (over 15 pounds) will only be there if they've been left alone. If you catch one or two "sow" snapper and then leave, you can return next month, or certainly the same time next year, for a couple more. However, if you catch a few limits of big ones, along with a few fat grouper, the big fish will leave and not return. It happens all the time. Better to probe for one or two good fish at each spot, either by motoring against the current slowly, or by drifting. That's a fairly light impact on each spot.

Many anglers have found spots they feel like they own, and will go to great lengths to keep secret. One captain says, "If you need to borrow my truck or even my boat, stop by for a visit. But if you want the GPS numbers to that

Finding the right spot and anchoring accurately above it takes experience, especially on days when wind and tide compete in different directions. Getting it right often means happy results like this moment. Bottom photo courtesy of Ralph Delph.

little piece of hard bottom I found 48 miles out, forget about it." Good spots don't come easy, and are worth protecting.

Fortunately for the beginning angler, there are many resources for finding starter fishing spots, often referred to as "numbers" (longitude and latitude coordinates, or older Loran-C numbers.) There are charts sold at tackle shops, free reef lists from coastal county agencies, fishing and dive club newsletters, and offshore lists published on the Internet. Two groups in Florida that build reefs and publish the numbers are Organization of Artificial Reefs (OAR) in Tallahassee, and the Jacksonville Offshore Fishing Club.

Begin with some published numbers for

The minute your bait hits bottom, you'd better be on point.

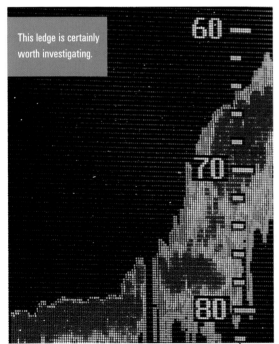

This ledge is certainly worth investigating.

your area, and then branch out from there, actively searching bottom while cruising or fishing offshore.

Rick Ryals has this advice: "When snapper fishing, it's a little difficult to explain what to look for on your bottom machine. One thing to avoid, though. You don't want a bunch of fish on your scope! The big ledges or wrecks with big marks of fish are almost always covered with bait and amberjack. We're after snapper, and certainly a few grouper. Give me a little crack in the bottom, or a patch of hard irregular bottom, marking just a few fish, and it's 'bombs away' for my crew."

GET READY

The anchor is finally set, and folks are grabbing baits and lowering them down. What next? A gag grouper will sometimes strike a live bait so hard it can rip a rod and reel from unsuspecting hands. Grouper fishing should preferably be done while standing. Captain Gary Folden has had several clients sitting on the edge of the boat, who were nearly pulled overboard by the strike of a powerful gag. "You can't catch a grouper sitting on your pooper," is one of his favorite slogans.

The first five seconds after a grouper has been hooked are critical. This part of the battle determines if the fish is going to "rock up" or not. With heavy tackle and the reel's drag screwed down, this really is man-versus-fish, and sometimes ladies too, a contest of who can out-muscle the other. It's also what makes grouper fishing so exciting. It's one thing to tangle with redfish on light tackle, but the full fury of a large grouper, or a large snapper for that matter, is something to experience.

A four-hour battle with a huge marlin is all about staying under control, and pacing yourself. A battle with a big grouper is all about the first few seconds. A snapper will run around the bottom until it gets tired, perhaps wrapping the line around something if it's lucky enough. But a big grouper is almost always within a few feet of his sanctuary. That means the minute your bait hits bottom, you'd better be on point. By the time you feel the bite, your grouper may be headed for home. Crank him up the first 10 or 15 feet, and he's on his way to your dinner table.

Amberjack are pretty good at breaking you off on bottom structure, but some of these grouper, especially the gag, wrote the book on that. It's important to anchor the right distance away. On the downside of a ledge, a gag can flare his gills underneath a rock no bigger than he is, and you can pull hard enough to turn your boat over, before he'll ever let go. Worse, there is evidence that when other gags notice this radical defensive behavior, they become extremely cautious and may decline all offerings.

What to do if you get out-muscled by a powerful fish in those first few seconds? Some fishermen pull hard against the stubborn fish until something gives. Other anglers keep a very tight line (wrapped around their fist) and then twang it like a banjo string. They claim the noise or vibration irritates the fish into coming out. Violently yanking the rod up and down sometimes works, but only as a last resort. Instead, try leaving the sinker resting on bottom so there is no tension on the fish. Keep the main line just tight enough to feel the sinker with no slack, and the rodtip almost touching the water. Wait patiently in this position for the fish to move, or vibrate the line, at which time you should lift the rod as quickly as possible.

If the fish is out of the rock, you'll feel the

Anchoring duty over a shallow wreck, in this case a hopper barge sunk close to the beach.

softer weight. Crank the reel as fast as possible, or he may return to the same hole. If you lift the rod and the fish remains in his lair, just set the sinker back on bottom and wait again for any sign of movement. Folks have waited out their "rocked up" grouper for up to 30 minutes and succeeded. Admittedly, such patience is difficult when other fish are biting fast. On the slow days, it's worth it. That may be a 15-pounder or possibly the day's best fish waiting at the end of the line.

Occasionally, a grouper is big and strong enough to leave his hole, power his way 20 feet or more to a better hideout, and repeat the performance. And this against 60-pound line, with a tight drag on the reel. These fish

Mark Your Spot

don't come easy; the same unlucky angler may hook five or 10 grouper and lose every one, simply because he lacks the upper body strength to stop them, and a good fish hideout happens to be mere feet away. Captain Kevin McMillan in Tarpon Springs reports seeing huge gags of at least 40 pounds lurking below his boat, sometimes following smaller 10-pounders that were hooked. When he managed to hook some of the bigger brutes only 10 feet under his boat, he was unable to stop them with 80-pound line; they still reached bottom in 40 feet and broke him off.

So you've found a spot, marked something promising on the bottom, and it's time to check it out. What next?

To mark your spot, many bottom fishermen use a small buoy, perhaps with a trigger mechanism to stop line from paying out after the weight strikes bottom. Using a heavy weight keeps your buoy from dragging in the current and losing the spot you just found. When the bottom machine begins to mark hard or broken bottom, throw the buoy and circle the area, until you decide exactly where to drop some baits.

Younger captains who grew up using a chart-

Anchoring near the marker buoy often results in a quick hookup. In calm conditions with a light current, the job is much easier.

Fishing over rock and coral guarantees you'll eventually hang hook or sinker on bottom, often thanks to a gag grouper. If the hook is merely snagged, you will be able to raise and lower the rod and feel the weight of the sinker going up and down. The best way to remedy this situation is to rest the sinker on bottom, bring the rod to a horizontal position approximately chest high, take out all the slack and "jag" the rod up and down—whap! whap!—

plotter may laugh at the buoy, but it gives a good idea of the current's velocity and direction, while marking the initial spot. It's a great, low-tech reference point on a featureless ocean. In the old days, the big boats used a buoy with a cane pole, topped with a flag. That's because they would range a quarter mile or more from their initial throw, and it's hard to spot anything less than a flag in 5- to 7-foot whitecaps, or worse. They didn't have precise electronics to guide them back to

See DVD for more tips on marking your spot.

Rick Ryals prpares to toss the buoy to mark his spot.

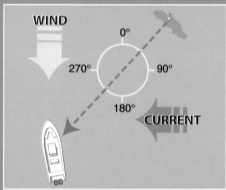

Boat drifts away from buoy, after first tossing it and returning within five feet of it. Drift direction is thus determined.

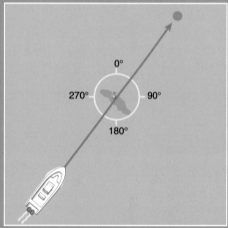

Swivel the boat and point straight at the buoy. Pass within five feet of it. Proceed on exact same compass heading.

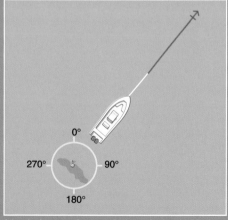

A hundred or more feet past the buoy, drop anchor. Back the boat up to the buoy, and tie off anchor line. Showtime.

their buoy. Some of today's captains prefer not to use a buoy on the weekend because it attracts passing boats. Others use a discreet, black, one-quart oil jug when they fish on weekends.

Once a crew decides to anchor on a spot, there's no more accurate way to gauge the current than to utilize a buoy. Nudge the bow of the boat a couple feet downcurrent of the buoy, and take the boat's engines out of gear. Then, wait a minute or two to drift a few yards with the current. Then, swivel the boat to point exactly at the distant, receding buoy, check your compass heading, drive straight to the buoy and beyond it, and then drop anchor. This is the same technique, basically, that you would use with a GPS unit: the navigation screen will tell you how fast and in what direction you are drifting away from your spot, and you can use that to run a reverse course upcurrent of the spot.

Dropping a certain distance from the buoy or mark will take a little practice. In a 10-knot wind with a moderate current, a rule of thumb would be to run three times the water's depth past the buoy, before dropping. If you estimated correctly, the

very rapidly. Many times this will dislodge the hook. If this fails or the fish that "rocked you up" refuses to cooperate, it's time to use the technique mentioned above, except jag the rod as hard as possible—bam! bam! This will usually cause the leader to chafe on a rock and break, or pop one of the knots.

If there is no sensation of the sinker flopping up and down, the sinker is wedged in rocks. Simply point the rod straight down in the water, tighten the line up, clamp a thumb on the reel spool, and pull straight up. Sometimes it will pop right out, or rip loose from soft coral or sponges. If not, pull even harder to force the knot to break at the sinker. As one may surmise, a lot of extra hooks and sinkers are required on these trips.

Perfect scenarios happen, when each

Gags and snapper sometimes just prefer large structures.

grouper is brought up without reaching his hideout. Other days the wind and current are at odds, or every gag you hook has only to pull a little belly out of the line (from the current) to work himself into a nice hole. When that happens, it's time to reposition the boat and coax those fish out across open sand a few feet. If not, it may be time to go trolling for pelagics. Or find some snapper, at least. On the Gulf side of Florida, folks have the option of trolling for the same grouper that are breaking them off. Not so on the Atlantic side. (See the trolling section).

Gags and snapper just sometimes prefer large, structured shelters. Ledges with big undercuts and heavy coral growth are a favorite. Unfortunately, such areas make it easy for these strong fish to race into a ledge or hole, where they can cut the line. Or more likely, they force an angler to break it off, after minutes of furious tugging against unyielding bottom. Gags are masters at this trick. Some days they'll leave a group of beaten, if not bruised anglers with an empty fishbox and a trip back to the tackle store. This would indicate either the boat was anchored too close to

Capt. Dennis Young hefts a gag and red snapper near his buoy, within sight of Mayport, Florida.

If you catch a good snapper while drifting, mark the spot with a buoy and anchor up for a half hour.

boat will settle on the anchor line close enough to actually lean over the side and pick up the buoy. There's no need to leave a buoy in the water that close to the boat. A big fish can easily wrap up in the buoy line. An approaching boat may call for a fast exit from a favorite honeyhole. A stowed buoy is one less headache, plus you won't forget it once you pull anchor to run for home.

You might want to drop a few baits before anchoring, depending on the time of year and bait availability. If it's spring or fall, and you have live cigar minnows, sardines or other prime baits, try sending a couple of them down to see what sort of fish are home that day. If you catch a good snapper while drifting, mark the spot and anchor. However, if it's winter, the water is cold, and all you have are frozen baits, it may be most efficient to anchor up right away. In winter, it takes longer for snapper and grouper to get the message that dinner is served. Drifting won't give much indication of what might actually be down there.

Better to anchor and be patient during winter. It may require a half-hour of chumming because of poor water visibility, or low water temperatures may keep the fish a bit sluggish. Gag grouper often need a half hour to wake up in winter. Even in warm weather, they have a curious habit of not biting for an hour or two, and then suddenly "turning on," with three or four fish hitting in rapid succession. Gags can be so finicky on some days, anglers may need to try six or eight kinds of bait before finally hooking a fish. For instance, those ladyfish caught earlier on the grassflats may be the only meal ticket for grouper. Drifting by a prime spot without anchoring may produce nothing, while patience and setting out a spread of baits while on anchor can produce some savage action. SB

Nice mix of North Florida red snapper, with keeper-sized, tasty seabass mixed in.

the angler much more of an advantage.

If your bait is not exactly where the grouper are, grunts and seabass will locate and begin tearing into it. This feeding activity will often cause grouper to wander over for a look. If a grouper is interested, he'll bully his way in and take the bait away from smaller fish. To begin this chain of events, and get some smell and fish fragments scattered on bottom, always start with some type of dead bait as the initial offering. Captain Folden says that only after he's caught several grouper on dead bait will he send down a valuable live bait for them to pounce on.

The nature of all grouper is to head for heavy cover the moment it feels a hook and realizes that something isn't right. This behavior is curious, because grouper can be bullies and are typically the top, day-time predator found on the reefs, if you subtract sharks. Why grouper run and hide so quickly when they feel a hook is a mystery. This behavior is what makes grouper so darn difficult to catch.

FINESSING BOTTOM FISH

Not all bottom fishing is about brute strength. If you're anchored or drifting very slowly, take your standard kingfish tackle (a light-tipped 6½-foot fiberglass stick with 20- to 30-pound test, and a high speed reel) and drop your favorite bait (more on that later) very slowly, using a 4-foot leader and a 3-ounce egg sinker. Get ready to learn some lessons about red snapper.

First, you'll learn that the stories about hooked snapper dragging big, brawny anglers to their knees are exaggerated. Big grouper and amberjack will dive under structure, and are certainly capable of these things. But snapper often fight with some elbow room, out in the open. Anglers learn this pretty quick when they scale back on heavy tackle. They get more hookups, too. The stealthy touch with lighter tackle doesn't alert the entire city of Atlantis that something is wrong with your bait.

Drop your lighter bait and weight down slowly and you'll also learn what divers have

Angler thumbs spool, to stop a big fish from reaching his lair.

the rock itself, or they were using tackle with inadequate stopping power.

Many anglers still prefer to anchor as close to the underwater wreck, rocks or ledge as possible, though preferably not straight above it. Ideally, one would chum these fish 30 to 40 feet away from their structure, before hooking them. This gives

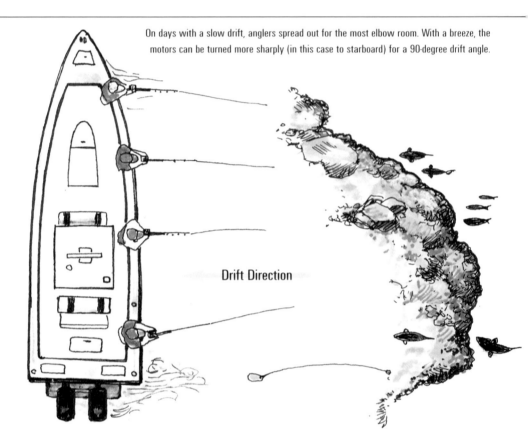

On days with a slow drift, anglers spread out for the most elbow room. With a breeze, the motors can be turned more sharply (in this case to starboard) for a 90-degree drift angle.

Drift Direction

always known. The biggest snapper are often found well up in the water column, sometimes far above the juveniles. A large percentage of the biggest snapper are hooked while slowly lowering a bait down through the depths.

When fishing heavy tackle, the pure strength of a big snapper is something to behold. Quite often a hook pulls out, or something breaks. Try hooking that same fish on 30-pound test, and you'll be surprised at how easy you'll beat him. Anglers really don't know if the heavy tackle panics these fish, or if the light tackle fools them into believing nothing is wrong. Regardless, on light tackle a big snapper is easier than one would think. One word of caution: Using a 40-pound leader means it gets significantly weakened with almost every fish. Be prepared to check your line often and use fresh leaders. As another benefit, the rod and reel combo weighs far less. The lighter drag and lead weight means less lifting. It makes for a more relaxing day with fewer bruises.

Handling a bite on light tackle involves a considerably different technique from heavy tackle. Two words are important here: "Just crank." When using a heavy rod, the age-old technique is to keep a tight line, ready to stab the rod skyward at the first hint of a bite. On lighter tackle, the fish probably won't even feel such fancy gyrations. It's far better to get that high-speed reel handle flying, and save your rod-jerk until the drag starts slipping. Either way, drop the bait deep until the sinker finds bottom. Remember to keep a tight line, with the sinker hovering inches off bottom. Make sure you stay in contact with the bottom until you feel a bite—until you're ready to reel in line. Once you feel a snapper pop the bait, you'll feel the steady tug as he starts away with it. That's the time to start cranking.

DRIFTING

Drift-fishing is an option in 80 feet of water or less, rather than a near-necessity, like it is in deep water (see chapter 3). For instance, drifting is highly recommended for red grouper fishing over live bottom off Florida's west coast. Why? Because these fish are normally dispersed and scattered across low-profile bottom. They live in hideyholes and dart out when a meal passes by. Drifting also works for red snapper when the current isn't too fast. Baits can be sent down on an exploratory basis

to see what's there, before going to the trouble of anchoring. Those fishing in deeper water, in 100 to 300 feet, do far more drift-fishing for snapper and grouper.

According to Jacksonville's Rick Ryals, there are several things wrong with drift-fish-

Anchoring Tips It's always best to get the anchoring

For recreational purposes, the most popular style of anchor is the Danforth. Its triangular flukes dig into sand and also grab well on rocky bottom. Choose the size of the anchor based on the size of your vessel; many boat stores can assist in that selection.

An anchor is nothing without a chain, however. The chain performs two critical functions. It prevents chafing from the rocks below, but it really helps in setting the anchor, by keeping a low angle on the shaft as it digs in. Five feet of good chain would be the minimum amount. Eight feet is better. And some specialists use 12 feet or more. Anchor line should be nylon and the diameter should match up with the boat's size and weight. Don't skimp on the length of the line. As an example, if you regularly fish in 50 feet of water, then 300 feet of anchor line would not be too much. Spools are available in that very length. Instead of one long anchor line,

Above, easily retrieved anchor with buoy attached. Below, 12 feet of steel anchor chain is very good insurance.

some anglers now connect 50- or 100-foot line sections with quick-release snaps, or carabiners. One can snap a buoy on the anchor line and dump it overboard when a fast exit is required.

Remember, if the motor won't start and you're far offshore, or even adrift near rocky jetties, you need a strong anchor, with sufficient line and chain that will hold you in position, not one that

See DVD for more tips on proper anchoring procedures.

ing for grouper in the Atlantic. "Most importantly, grouper feed slower than snapper," he says. This might be because they generally don't travel in big schools, making for less competition. Whatever the reason, gags usually feed much slower than drift-fishing will

allow. Anglers may feel like they're making a slow drift with baits, but a glance at the marker buoy reveals just how fast the boat is drifting, usually too fast for grouper. You may think your baits are sitting still, but the truth is, they're flying across the sand faster than a gag wants to chase after them.

procedure right the first time.

skips merrily along the bottom, leaving the boat at the mercy of wind and tide. One more reminder: Always tie off the "bitter end" (the end opposite the anchor) to something solid inside the anchor locker.

★★★★ **Always make sure the boat is backing down as the anchor rope pays out. This will prevent the anchor, chain and line from ending up in a big heap on rocky bottom, where it can tangle and snag. As the boat backs, let the anchor line ride through your hand while giving mild resistance. This will cause the anchor to turn and rest on bottom in a position ready to dig in, with the anchor's flukes pointing toward the boat.**

Try to get the anchoring procedure right the first time. That means setting the anchor firmly, with sufficient line so it won't drag. This is especially important when anchoring over a prime honeyhole. Many of the best anglers feel that dragging an anchor through a school of snapper or grouper will scatter them like chickens, a detriment to a good day's catch. A successful first attempt may not earn respect or salutations from nearby boats fishing the same spot, such as a big artificial reef. But if you repeatedly drag anchor through the fleet because of inadequate bottom gear, expect some derision and scorn from nearby boats within hailing distance. SB

JIGGING

There are situations offshore where jigging works very well in depths of 80 feet or less. A 2-ounce jig tipped with a fresh sardine or cigar minnow may be slammed by red snapper only 40 or 50 feet below the surface, when drifting past Gulf wrecks, rocks, oil or gas platforms and towers. During summer, it's best to miss the hard structure by at least 30 yards and often more when the current is slow. Why? Triggerfish will sprint from cover to chase after any fresh or frozen meat, where they usually steal it. The snapper range out farther away from structure, farther even than amberjack. The jig has an advantage over bare hooks. If you miss a strike and lose the bait off a jig, you can still dance it around a few times in 2- or 3-foot yanks, and earn another strike. A lot of big red snapper have been taken on baitless jigs in this way. And, there are many fine bonus fish (cobia, kingfish, mahi and amberjack) happy to slam a lively jig when a snapper or grouper won't.

Boat anchored sideways in gentle current. Each angler can better reach the spot.

The Florida Keys is something of a different situation from the rest of the Southeast or Gulf Coast states. Close proximity to land, clear water and almost all of the shallow coral in the U.S. are packed into a relatively small area. Some of it can be fished visually without relying on electronics, and certainly was for many years. After all, a dark patch of bottom in these waters means either coral or a wreck down below. Anchor up and chum an acre of multi-colored bottom in 30 feet of water, surrounded by brilliant white sand tinted green by the water, and you'll likely start catching fish. The GPS does make it easier to approach that favorite patch reef efficiently, perhaps in a stealthy manner from upwind. Some anglers with twin-engine boats even make the approach with one engine turned off, cutting underwater noise in half. In deeper water of 60 to 80 feet, bottom details are more vague, making electronic navigation more necessary. Accurate use of this equip-

Boat positioning is the ticket here. The ideal patch reef is 20 to 40 feet deep, separate from the main reef mass.

ment and anchoring skills in these depths are almost as necessary as outside the Keys, where bottom features are seldom if ever visible.

Here's what Capt. George Mitchell, our Keys expert, has to say about fishing the Keys patch and coral reefs:

"Boat positioning is once again the ticket here. The ideal patch reef is 20 to 40 feet deep, surrounded by a sand ring and deep, lush seagrass. It should be separate from the main reef mass. Even better would be a reef that has

more structure just downcurrent. You can spend an entire day at one reef, or decide to move around, but give each spot at least an hour of patience. A little reminder: These fish can turn on just as easily as they turn off. However, a surefire way to shut down the action is to break off a fish in the reef, and leave him with a good length of line trailing behind him. Also, if you've hooked into a good fish that has jumped into a hole, don't give up right away; it has to come out at some

Angler on the stern deals with yellowtail snapper feeding in the chum line, far behind. He's using lighter tackle and small baits. Below the boat, a bigger mutton snapper has taken a bigger bait on bottom. The boat is anchored properly over sand.

point. I know one junior angler who waited out a red grouper for over an hour, before coaxing him to the boat.

"With a bait on bottom, it's best to keep the rod as close to horizontal as possible, and as soon as the fish bites, reel fast. A friend of

Happy young angler with rock hind grouper caught from shallow coral reef.

mine named Capt. Mark Krowka coined the phrase, 'Reel at the speed of light, times two!' Once the fish is glued on, you can utilize a rod belt or other gut-saving device, but the first few feet are critical in a mutton snapper battle. A steady pump-and-reeling technique is fine once

you have cleared the fish from structure, but after that, slow down. If there are underwater predators around, they will attack the faster fish first. Also, snapper tend to swell as their swim bladders expand, and they'll quit fighting halfway up. You don't want to be jigging a 3-pound mutton snapper or yellowtail in front of a hungry barracuda," Mitchell said.

That clear Keys water does come in handy for setting out an accurate spread of bottom baits. Where else can you set baits precisely, within two feet of structure? Only The Bahamas and Caribbean have similar water in this hemisphere.

"I like to put a baited rig on each side of the patch reef, just outside the sand ring, and one down the middle a little closer to the rocks. The outside baits (see bait chapter) will be rigged with No. 3 wire between the two hooks, on a short, 2-foot section of leader. A No. 5 swivel keeps the lead from sliding down to the bait. You'll need different size leads, depending on wind and current. The wire-equipped baits should be fished with the spinning reel's bails closed, while the center, single-hooked, mono leader bait will have a slight dropback. With some baits we pin the hooks to the top side, others on the bottom. Usually the bottom-hooked baits are fished closer to the reef, while those hooked in the top of the tail are fished outside the sand ring in the grass bottom.

Keep in mind that when fishing with small, live pilchards you will need to scale down the leader size, to match water clarity and current conditions. The lightest line we use is 20-pound. You have to pull hard, to keep these fish away from coral bottom." SB

Anchoring on the Patches

Be *sure* you don't drop the anchor on coral.

Drop only in the light-colored sandy areas, away from the reef.

If another boat isn't anchored nearby, I like to observe the way a lobster trap buoy lays in the water nearby, to figure out the way the boat will sit on anchor. Once you can physically see the reef, it's time to "form the question mark." I named it that because from above, your propwash creates a big question mark with the reef or fishing spot in the middle. You get close, ID the spot visually, and then circle it half-way before anchoring. Be absolutely sure you are not dropping anchor on the actual coral. This causes damage to precious fish habitat that grows very slowly. Drop anchor only in the light-colored sandy areas, away from the reef.

If you are going to fish what we call the "finger channels," try to have the wind and tide in your favor. An incoming tide seems to be best, because it allows chum to flow into the grassflats where ballyhoo live. Look for a channel that has a steady depth, and then a deeper hole. I like an area that provides a break in the current. Ledges and potholes in the channels are also great. Anchor the boat upcurrent of the target zone, preferably over grassy bottom. It's best to approach your spot from upcurrent, but if you have to drive right over it, go slowly.

As for the best depths for yellowtail, I prefer 40 to 60 feet. It seems like you can always find fishable water at that depth. Some anglers don't like much current, and will anchor in shallower water to escape that. It's best to have the wind and current working together, but the most important thing is current. Typically the closer you get to the full or new moon, the stronger the current. Yellowtail snapper are a wary bunch, and won't venture far from safety when there is no current. But the current will also spread your chum slick across more bottom, attracting more fish into the strike zone. SB

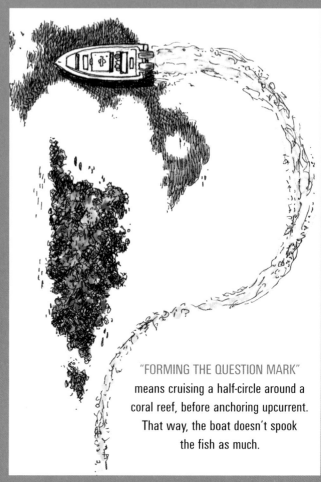

"FORMING THE QUESTION MARK" means cruising a half-circle around a coral reef, before anchoring upcurrent. That way, the boat doesn't spook the fish as much.

Locating Red Grouper Over "Swiss Cheese" Limestone Bottom

Much of the Gulf of Mexico is relatively flat, compared to the Atlantic. So, when you're targeting red grouper on very small ledges that resemble holes, your search is completely different from searching for gags and blacks on bigger ledges.

STEP 1. Try to locate the transition area between hard bottom and sand. The transition area holds more fish than other areas of hard bottom. Look for the thickening (actually fish) of bottom that corresponds with a tailing mark and the appearance of the second echo.

STEP 2. If you have a GPS with a plotter, hit the Event, Instant Store or Man Overboard key. If you don't have a plotter, throw a buoy as you mark good hard bottom with signs of fish.

STEP 3. In most cases, your drift won't be too fast, so it's best to drift your spot and drop a few baits. Smelly dead baits such as squid or cut sardines work perfectly here.

STEP 4. If you catch a sub-legal grouper it may be a good idea to anchor, but in many cases veteran grouper diggers won't anchor until they catch at least one keeper grouper.

STEP 5. For two reasons, it's good to move to another spot after catching three or four legal red grouper. The most important reason is that your odds of catching more are pretty slim. Secondly, if you do hit a real honeyhole that produces a half dozen or more grouper, you'll want to save a few hungry fish for your next trip.

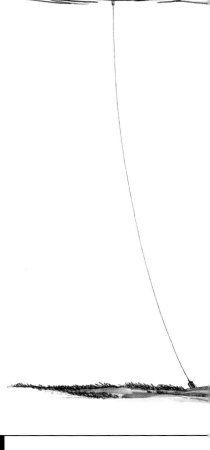

Limestone Formations

LEDGES

These are almost certainly the most productive natural structure offshore. A ledge is a sudden rise of rock from the sandy bottom, the height of which may be from one to five feet, though they can tower much higher along some sections of the coast. Ledges are often undercut, providing a rocky overhang for grouper, snapper, even lobster. This is easily recognized on a bottom machine, which may explain why it remains the most popular natural bottom.

ROCKPILES

Also known for holding good fish. In the Florida Keys and Bahamas, they're called coral heads, because coral is usually attached. When completely coated with marine growth, they can be impressive structures to fish. Elsewhere, rockpiles are often rather simple formations, nothing more than a group of boulders sitting in the sand and yet, they still attract plenty of fish.

Drifting over flat, Swiss cheese rock bottom. Such spots attract both red and gag grouper, along with grunts and some seabass.

FLAT ROCK OR HARD BOTTOM

These sometimes have large cracks running through them. The upper portion of the rock grows sponges and corals, but it is the cracks where grouper and snapper hang out. This bottom is very difficult to spot on a bottom machine and is often only noticed by a slight show of fish just off bottom. Often the only sign is a thick readout on the bottom line of the recorder, with no fish. Anchoring and chumming will attract them, however.

SWISS CHEESE

This is another formation frequently referred to as hard bottom. These are areas where flat limestone has eroded, creating small "solution" holes. The holes are not large or deep, but they still provide safety and cover that grouper and snapper prefer. Were you to view these from above, they might resemble a slice of Swiss cheese. As one may imagine, they're difficult to decipher on a depth recorder.

CHAPTER 4

Deeper Reefs and Ledges

Ever try fishing in deeper water, out beyond the typical partyboat depths of a hundred feet or so? Drop baits in 200 or 300 feet, and you'll likely catch not only bigger fish, but perhaps a few species of snapper or grouper new to you and the crew. As bottom fish mature, they usually move offshore into these same depths of water, and that's where you'll find tasty silk snapper or yellowfin and scamp grouper, to name but a few.

Sure, it's more work pulling up fish from those depths, but the quality of those fish is worth the effort. Especially if you don't have to run 50 to 100 miles offshore, like many anglers do.

Sure, it's more work, but the quality of those fish is worth the effort.

Tropical, yellowfin grouper caught in 200 feet off Louisiana. This is a popular fish in The Bahamas, but they will stray across the Gulf.

Probing the Deeper Reefs

Anglers who bottom fish out beyond 80 feet, to perhaps 250 feet, have a different set of challenges to overcome. The deeper water makes anchoring accurately over a small spot almost problematical, for instance. Shifting winds and currents and their interplay mean that many boat captains much prefer to drift or motor-fish over these spots, making repeated passes, dropping baited hooks.

The rewards of fishing deeper water are certainly worth the effort, because virtually all species of bottom fish, when they grow larger, move into deeper water.

For instance, if you're targeting a "copperbelly" gag grouper in excess of 20 pounds, you would normally fish deeper than 100 feet, and much closer to 200 feet. Ditto for outsize mutton and red snapper. It's the same with jumbo red and black grouper, though black grouper do migrate near shallower reefs in winter. But the rewards can be great for fishing deeper water during the entire year.

For one thing, you won't have temperature changes to contend with. The heat of summer and the cold fronts of winter simply do not penetrate 200 feet below the surface. It's a fairly stable environment that big fish prefer. So, this is not a seasonal fishery. It's a year-round thing with special techniques worth knowing. The deeper spots have been fished far less by the weekend crowds, and finding one can mean hitting the jackpot.

A good bottom machine set on the bottom zoom function is essential. With plenty of power, of course, something in the range of 1,000 watts. There is little need to see fish more than 30 feet above bottom, so zooming in on the bottom 30 feet for the entire viewing screen is the best way to reveal bottom irregularities and fish. Marking the entire 200 feet of

Above, depthfinder marks an 80-foot peak rising from deeper water. This is bound to be a place worth checking out. At left, this angler cranked up a doubleheader in 190 feet during a late summer "night bite." He has a possible world record red hind, along with a typical red snapper from those depths.

This tremendous, 52-pound "copperbelly" gag grouper was caught with 10-pound spin tackle.

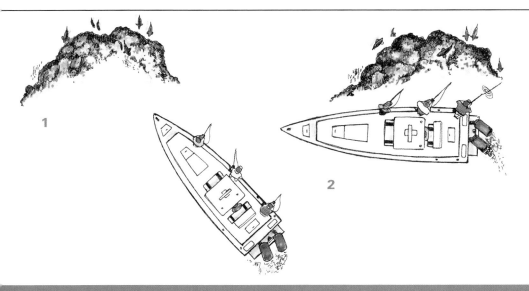

(1) This boat approaches a deep rock with all three anglers on the starboard side. (2) As the boat pivots, the stern-most angler walks to port, keeping his line clear of the motors. (3) The captain then points the stern back at the spot,

This angler baited up with two baits, using live vermilion snapper. He landed this warsaw grouper.

water column is fruitless for two reasons: The fish are on bottom, and the wide display shrinks anything on bottom until it's too small to even notice.

There are boating techniques for fishing this deeper water. Picking a spot is fine, but you don't want to simply toss the anchor upwind of the buoy and hope for the best. That often results in having the anchor line tighten up too far from the buoy to effectively fish. Repeated anchoring corrections in 200 feet may be enough to incite a mutiny, without some good fish being caught. As the old-timers know, manually pulling an anchor and chain up from those depths is what they call "man-killer" work.

Still, accurately landing baits on a small bottom target can be a problem, no matter how easy it is to drop anchor and retrieve.

Many anglers instead prefer to drift or "motor fish" with the engines idling, occasionally bumping the engines into gear to slow down the drift when the current is moving. If the current is strong, heavier lead weights are a must, and it's a day-long struggle for the captain to accurately place his baits on the fish.

In some parts of the Gulf and Atlantic, a couple of large red snapper in 200 feet may inhabit a rock only as big as a car. When the current is still, one merely has to park the boat

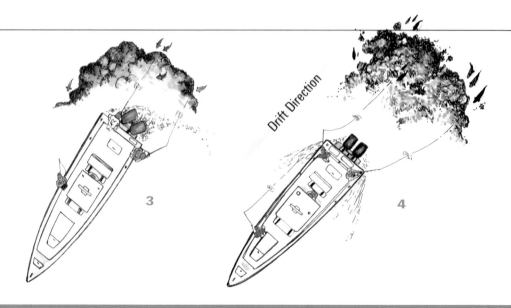

Drift Direction

3

4

Far below, the three live pinfish are being inspected by good-sized black and gag grouper and mutton snappers.

overhead. If it's ripping and the wind is blowing, it's much tougher to reach.

A number of veteran bottom fishermen in this deeper water merely rig up for big red snapper with a dropper rig, consisting of a 16-ounce sinker and a whole cigar minnow. Red snapper are not the brightest fish in the Gulf, and often do not require rigs such as long leaders on a 3-way swivel or sliding egg sinker rigs. These tiny rock spots have fewer triggerfish and bait stealers, so a frozen cigar minnow works fine on a short leader. It's best in many cases to merely reel fast, to take up a dozen feet of slack and line stretch, counting on today's extra-sharp hooks (often chemically sharpened) to set themselves. Before these J-hooks became popular, many used circle hooks, counting on the fish to hook themselves. If the fish weren't that hungry it was difficult to catch them, since it takes an aggressive fish to hook itself on a circle hook.

In South Florida and the Keys, where deep water is easily within sight of land, dropping baits in 150 to 250 feet is an everyday affair, weather permitting. Several bottom rig options can be used (see that chapter), but some of the better snapper and grouper anglers seem to prefer the same drift technique. They keep their engines running, using occasional power to slow down the drift, backing into the current or waves, whichever is dominant.

It's actually a little more complicated than that. Use your GPS to assess the direction and speed of the drift, then pick an imaginary drop that will allow the baits to sink for a minute or two as you drift by the spot. That drop spot may be closer to the target on slow current days, and farther with a stronger current. Some boat crews simply follow this procedure, stop the engines and drift-fish. But not everyone.

HERE'S HOW SOME OF THE PROS DO IT

As the X spot is reached (approaching from the side), pivot the boat 90 degrees, presenting the stern to the current or wind, whichever is more dominant. As the boat begins to pivot, the stern angler on the inside of the pivot point (who has a live bait nose-hooked, resting in a bucket) needs to drop his bait deep. Roughly 10 seconds later, after the boat has pivoted 90 degrees, its time for the angler on the

Another massive black grouper caught on 20-pound braided line, using 6- to 9-ounce jigs. Photo courtesy of Ralph Delph.

other side of the stern to make his drop. The two baits go deeper, one at least 50 feet ahead of the other, the baits dragged down by 6-ounce egg sinkers on a normal day, and 8-ounce sinkers or more on a day with stronger currents or wind. Once these two baits near bottom, it's time to yell for the third angler, who is 20 feet forward (toward the bow, of course) to drop his bait. A fourth angler isn't used, as it's felt that four lines in the water is too much.

The boat settles down with its stern to the wind or current, the captain bumping the engines into reverse as conditions call for, to slow the drift and keep the baits over what may be a small spot. Far below, the three live pinfish are being inspected by good-sized black and gag grouper, or mutton snapper. Detecting a bite takes a keen eye with monofilament. Often it's just a small, telltale nod or two of the rodtip. That's the signal to being reeling fast. If the rod bends enough to signify a fish, one option is to gently gun the boat ahead at least 20 feet, which gives the fish below a mighty pull away from his lair. As the fight progresses, the boat is allowed to drift along without being slowed, and thus the grouper or snapper is pulled along even more by the weight of the boat, which is pushed by wind and tide.

This angler works patiently on a big Nassau, the dominant grouper in The Bahamas. The Nassau is protected in Florida waters and should be reintroduced.

Detecting a bite when using monofilament takes a keen eye. Often it's just a telltale nod or two of the rodtip.

In this way, grouper up to 60 pounds are caught with only 30-pound line, an amazing thing to watch. In some cases, these fish are hooked close to their rocky homes and are quick enough to bolt back inside. Gunning the boat with a tightened drag may actually pull the fish out. This technique works well even on repeat customers; its not unusual to catch a black or gag grouper with last week's hook and leader still in its mouth.

Tackle for this sort of work isn't some huge reel with a pool cue rod. Medium tackle is fine and much easier to handle. Captain

Jack Carlson in Marathon is quite adept at this deeper fishing; he spends most of his days doing this in blue and sometimes choppy water.

Accompanying Jack on a trip around a deep rubble pile donated by the old Seven-Mile Bridge (we could plainly see the new bridge on the distant horizon), several boats there were drifting sideways or even anchored, dropping small blue crabs for permit that habitually school around there at mid-depth. Jack fishes the same spot, but somehow manages to pluck nice black grouper from the bottom using live pinfish. When we dropped ⅜-ounce bullet jigs with live blue crabs, on 12-pound spin tackle,

Fishing the bridge rubble reef off Marathon: Drop a small crab down on a weighty little jig while looking for permit, and look what happens!

more than 6 pounds. (Often mistakenly called "hog snapper," they're really a member of the wrasse family, rarely caught on hook and line. They're also a great prize on the dinner table.)

When currents are light and sharp dropoffs common, an alternate drift technique is to position over a rock perhaps in 150 feet and drift slowly into deeper water, reeling the lines back in after passing 250 feet, and repositioning for another drift. The boat itself may drift sideways in a light current and wind, moving slowly. (You can turn the still motors sharply as if turning the boat into the wind to achieve a perfect broadside drift, 90 degrees to the wind, which

in an effort to hook a permit, we were hit instead with several mutton snapper. A live shrimp on the same jig then produced a 15-pound Almaco jack, which fed six people that night in a local restaurant, and also a hogfish of

spreads the lines as far apart as possible. That means fewer lines tangling.) With a center console boat of 30 feet and longer, five anglers from bow to stern can lower baits down without tangling too often. The fifth angler or even a sixth can cast weightless live baits from the bow for bonus fish near the surface—mostly kingfish, blackfin tuna and cero mackerel.

This is also where deep-jigging earns its good name, with anglers probing these deeper spots with a 3- to 9-ounce spearhead, arrowhead or other jig with a plastic twister tail to provide a lifelike wiggle. No-stretch braided line is ideal for working the jig near bottom; a 3-foot sweep of the rod will make that jig pop up exactly three feet, even in 200 feet of water. That sweeping action is essential for giving life (or the appearance of it) to a chunk of lead and artificial tail material. A fairly stiff rod is required for this kind of work; you don't want a whippy rod or even a soft rodtip robbing motion from that jig. Multiple strikes are possible, so keep working the jig until something solid latches on.

A bite on a jig often translates to mere resistance on the rodtip, which requires fast reeling and a very sharp hook. It's amazing how powerful black grouper up to 60 pounds are caught this way from reefs in the Keys, on small reels filled with only 15-pound line.

Who would do such a thing?

Bill Prahl of Miami has been deep-jigging for more than 20 years, and prefers it over all other methods for catching snapper and grouper. His boat is designed for drift-fishing. It's a double-hulled catamaran, a stable plat-

As explained in our black grouper section, targeting these huge fish in the Keys means dropping a 6- to 9-ounce white jig down on braided, 20-pound line. A "twister" type of worm tail that glows in the dark adds life to the jig. It doesn't seem possible, but these huge grouper are somehow defeated with light tackle.

At left, a variety of big jigs exists for this work, many of them made in South Florida. Instead of jigging hard all day, anglers merely lift and lower the jig up and down, waiting for the slightest tap, which braided line is quick to detect.

These fish are normally caught while drift-fishing, but not always. Grouper photo courtesy of Ralph Delph.

form that doesn't rock much while drifting sideways to the wind.

His light tackle certainly works, too. Prahl feels that using 15- to 20-pound spin tackle is best for deep-jigging, using jigs of two ounces or less, in depths out to 250 feet. He uses graphite rods because they're lighter and more sensitive to strikes.

"It's easier on the arms, using this lighter gear," he says. "It's also sportier, draws more bites from fish, and doesn't wear the angler out, as heavier gear will. There are guys who work a 6-ounce jig with 50-pound braided line all day, often in deeper water than I fish. That sounds like work."

Fishing the wrecks is more difficult with

That's the beauty of deep-jigging, probing the water column and never knowing what will hit next. Yellowfin grouper above came from 175 feet.

lighter gear, because a sunken ship offers taller cover for the fish. That's when Prahl grabs his heavier, 20-pound tackle. He does feel the well-publicized wrecks receive far more fishing pressure, so he prefers drifting over deep reefs that only rise a few feet. The fish aren't so used to seeing jigs and hooks, and they have less cover to dart into.

"I've been using spin reels with monofilament for so long, I haven't even bothered to switch to the braided lines. I'm just used to it. I'm sure it stretches on the strike, but that's okay. I use a very stiff, 7-foot rod that can sweep the jig up and down, and that's important for setting the hook.

"Marshall King in Miami was a pioneer in deep-jigging, and I learned it from him," says Prahl. "He was one of the top fishermen in Miami before the days of GPS. He could really line up a distant shoreline, to re-find his reef spots. He preferred jigs of two ounces or less. And no anchoring.

"That's the beauty of deep-jigging, you never know what will hit them. You're fishing the entire water column, picking up bonus fish such as kingfish or cobia. The key to jigging is the territory you cover. The fish are spread out. There are spots along the reef that offer sustained action. Jigging may be more work, but it keeps you busy, and you're not just standing there waiting for a bite."

Many fishermen seem to prefer white jigs for deep-jigging, but Prahl says yellow may work better about 25 percent of the time. He uses two or three trailer hooks on his jigs, with a ballyhoo attached. He says fresh bait isn't always best; a fresh pack of frozen ballyhoo remains his favorite. He says a fresh ballyhoo or cigar minnow is too firm compared to frozen and thawed, and the hooks do stay in the bait better. Sometimes too well; they may not wind up in some reef predator's mouth as well as hoped for.

Many anglers may prefer to use a plain, or pure jig for various reasons. Some feel the unbaited jig performs better in the water column, hopping attractively with each pump of the rodtip. Others may wish to delete natural bait to foster a sense of personal accomplishment or perhaps fulfill a fishing club challenge. Classic deep-jigging, for many, means just that: fishing a jig and nothing else.

Prahl's best fish was a 60-pound black grouper, caught on 20-pound line. The fight took over a half hour, the fish hooked at a wreck in 200 feet of water. The fish was quickly released; Prahl says they had no use for a grouper of that size, and the smaller ones taste better anyway.

That's a pretty sound endorsement for fishing out beyond where most folks anchor and bottom fish. The technique works; it seems that Prahl has released bigger grouper than most anglers have ever caught.

Can't tell the difference between two grouper cousins? That's a black grouper on top, gag grouper on bottom.

CHAPTER 5

Fishing Wrecks & Artificial Reefs

F ew things are more exciting than getting the "numbers" to a wreck offshore, one that few boats have ever fished, and then actually finding it. The only thing better would be to stumble over a completely new wreck covered with fish, something that happens to fishermen every year. After all, many unfortunate vessels have gone down in the past 200 years, and most became havens for fish. Some are still undiscovered and remain the ultimate prize. Public artificial reefs aren't quite that romantic; they're more the bread and butter reefs that serve the public so well on a weekly basis, when the weather permits.

Bottom fish prefer a hole almost anywhere along the side of a wreck. They may also prefer the stern, around the propellers.

Big black grouper patrols a wreck in tropical waters. This sailboat has been on the bottom for quite some time, a haven for fish. Underwater photos courtesy of Charlotte Lloyd and Don DeMaria.

Advice on Artificial Reefs

Some captains really do prefer the smaller wrecks, from 30 to 80 feet long.

Pulling snapper and grouper from wrecks and artificial reef piles is a little different from natural bottom, and perhaps more seasonal. Off Jacksonville, there are something like 300 sites offshore. These are

bridge concrete: these guys have done it all.

We talked to a couple of area fishermen who have been around the Jacksonville offshore scene for 30 years, who have spent countless days fishing around these huge, submerged obstacles.

The approaches they use are duplicated elsewhere by experienced wreck fishermen. The biggest mistake fishermen make around wrecks is to anchor right on top of them. This is a multiple mistake. Why? If you drop anchor into the wreck, you may not get it back. Lose your primary (if not only) anchor offshore, and you've just cut your day short. While fishing on a short rope, you may be constantly snagging the structure below. With a nautically correct scope of seven feet of anchor line per foot of depth, you'll likely swing far from the

Happy anglers examine their fish, caught from a wreck in The Bahamas.

scattered along 80 miles of coast from Saint Augustine to Fernandina, and run offshore up to 31 miles in deeper water. They were built by the Jacksonville Offshore Fishing Club, and it's difficult to imagine any other group in the country that has been so instrumental in developing so large an area for bottom fishing. Ships, barges, tugboats, concrete culverts,

wreck. Too close, if you hook a big fish, it likely has an easy time wrapping around structure. If you manage to horse it up, a pack of summertime barracuda might rip it to shreds. Did we mention that big bottom fish aren't even on the structure, but lurking over sand along both sides, or the ends?

To avoid all these problems, let's go over

some proper techniques for anchoring around wrecks and artificial reefs. Keep in mind in some areas that it's best to fish wrecks when the water isn't so warm and the barracuda have migrated to warmer climes.

Toss a marker buoy or get a fix on your GPS, circle the mark and scope out the length and width of the site. Watch for holes, dips in the sand scoured by a current washout. This is often where bottom fish congregate. If you mark a wad or stack of big fish, make a note of it. Then, drop anchor upcurrent of the chosen spot, back down and tie the anchor rope off while still at least 20 or 30 feet upcurrent—perhaps farther in deeper water. If a big fish is hooked, it can be pulled at an angle away from the reef. This may be heavy work, and many fishers opt for 80-pound line. Always carry a heavy outfit or two onboard, especially when wreck fishing—some of these structures tower above bottom, offering a big grouper repeated shots at gaining cover.

Captain Dennis Young of Jacksonville, who fishes every day the weather is agreeable, says he prefers wrecks between 30 and 80 feet long. With the really big wrecks, the ships and bigger barges, fish are scattered, only staying on certain points of

Fishing the wrecks in summer may result in maimed gamefish, thanks to passing sharks or residential barracuda.

"I stay away from these wrecks in summer, because of the predators." Dennis Young

it. He shakes his head at the idea of fishing a sunken aircraft carrier, which is 800 feet long. He thinks it will take years before something like that is good for bottom fishing. It's the same with Liberty shipwrecks, since they were more than 600 feet long.

He says certain fish congregate together, and bottom fish might hide on one small part of a big wreck. Amberjack roam the entire wreck, of course, along with barracuda and kingfish. But snapper and grouper often take

up only certain spots. They'll move around the wreck as the seasons change, but only inhabit a small area. On one ship, they may stay around the propellers only. They may hang around the bow of the ship if there is a washout. They also favor a hole anywhere in the side of the ship.

"I stay away from these wrecks in the summer, because of the predators," said Young. "It's such a waste, releasing small fish there. And the big fish get eaten. I have much better luck

Artificial Reefs as

on natural bottom in summer. In late fall to early spring, the crowds, barracudas and bait-stealing triggerfish are gone, even most of the amberjack. That's when I can really look for big snapper and grouper at these artificial reefs."

Young likes the washouts next to wrecks, holes in the sand. But they shift from one storm to the next. If you have 15-foot seas for a few days, then the wreck is changed.

Catamaran boat anchored over artificial reef.

Especially the older wrecks, which deteriorate in storms. If the water depth is inside 80 feet, storms really affect them. In deeper water of perhaps 300 feet, the wrecks don't move at all. Prime washout holes are based on how the local currents strike each wreck. And on how the wreck sits. If a wreck points east and west, the hole will be on the south side, because strong currents typically come from the north off Jacksonville. This varies, of course, from region to region. If the wreck is closer to the beach, that's different. Inshore depths have the coastal current, and they move a lot. That can cause changes weekly.

Wrecks often attract hordes of bait-stealing triggerfish in summer, especially in the Gulf. They may be so bad that it necessitates fishing at night, when all triggers sleep. Anchoring 100 feet from a wreck won't make any difference—the triggerfish will chase after any meaty bait, right up to the

"Every artificial reef has some advantage," says Steve Parks, who is often underwater, observing the many reefs built off Jacksonville for the past 30 years. What he means is, each site has marine life to view. It might not always be snapper or grouper, but rather a baitfish cloud, or tropical fish. There's a different mix of fish at each spot, different dynamics. You might see a tropical fish mixed in, like a large, flag yellowtail swimming in a school of red snapper. It's up to fishermen to pick out the best artificial reefs with bottom fish.

For instance, a sunken tugboat lasts longer than a barge. Tugs are more strongly built with less water circulation, while a barge will eventually collapse into a heap of rusty plates, especially when pounded by a storm. Tugs are far shorter than barges, so the fish aren't so scattered out. If you make a good anchor-set with a tug a few feet away, your hooks will be close to the fish. Sunken barges and tugs also provide habitat for baitfish, but they also attract everything else, all sorts of predators both high and low in the water column.

Concrete culverts last longer than any steel wreck, probably centuries. They're nearly impervious to salt water, very heavy, and not easily moved by a storm. If they're stacked properly, really piled up, that's good for the grouper. If the culverts are scattered and spread out across the sand, that's not so good. It's best to search for the pileups.

Parks also agrees that a piece of aluminum from an airplane, even a 20-foot wing, will almost always be loaded with snapper, especially if there is a hole in the sand beside or beneath it. Captain Dennis Young says it's weird, but snapper lay their side to it and rub off a cloud of aluminum. Then they seem to inhale the powder. At least, they did on the wing off an older plane he inspected at 95 feet. The Navy used to dump excess material on the way back to port, sometimes close enough to shore where anglers could find it. Marine growth doesn't attach to aluminum, because it steadily corrodes. And the snappers were wearing their tails off on it. Nobody knows why.

On other wreck material as well, a natural washout hole can make a huge difference. Many bottom fish spend the night in those holes as protection against sharks. A lot of fish will fit in one hole, too. Sometimes an entire school of grouper will disappear down the same hole as a predator approaches. Grouper seem to prefer natural sand and rock holes (and freshwater spring holes) more than the inside of a wreck, but a wreck will do. They also love intact, concrete culverts; they know if a predator threatens them from one end, they can always exit the other side. Of course, a baitfish cloud overhead makes this scenario complete, since grouper have to eat. They can find sustenance around the bottom, but a cloud of sardines, cigar minnows or other silvery baitfish is the ticket to fast action.

Mangrove snapper appreciate a good hole as well, but they like the complete protection from the inside of a sunken boat. The wheelhouse on a shrimpboat or tugboat is perfect, if a door or window was left open. Mangroves hole up during the day in the offshore wrecks, and then they prowl around at night. Divers report during daylight hours, they see almost 100 percent of all mangrove snapper at a wreck stuffed inside, while red snapper all remained outside. That's something to consider when choosing tackle and baits.

Young said the steel wrecks attract almost all of the goliath grouper off Northeast Florida, and they've made a tremendous comeback. One goliath that weighs hundreds of pounds, that lives inside a wreck, is now reportedly too huge to escape through the only hole available. SB

Above, big dog snapper inside a wreck. Below, goliath grouper in artificial reef.

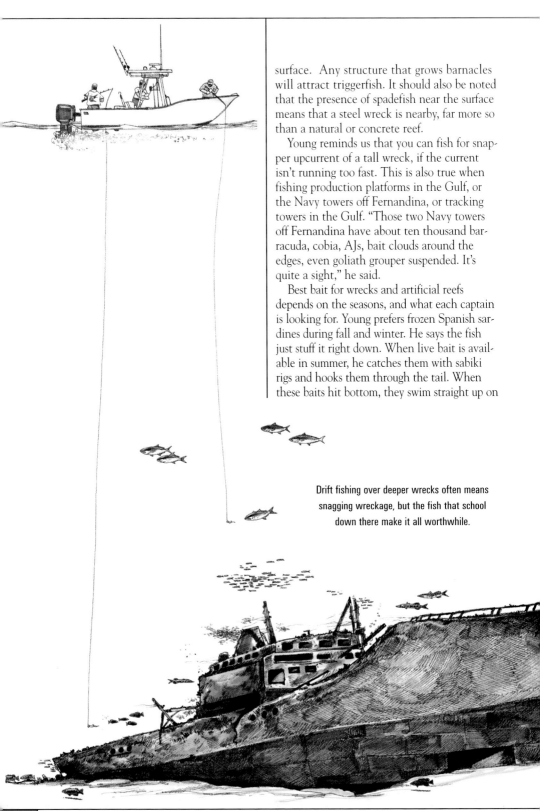

surface. Any structure that grows barnacles will attract triggerfish. It should also be noted that the presence of spadefish near the surface means that a steel wreck is nearby, far more so than a natural or concrete reef.

Young reminds us that you can fish for snapper upcurrent of a tall wreck, if the current isn't running too fast. This is also true when fishing production platforms in the Gulf, or the Navy towers off Fernandina, or tracking towers in the Gulf. "Those two Navy towers off Fernandina have about ten thousand barracuda, cobia, AJs, bait clouds around the edges, even goliath grouper suspended. It's quite a sight," he said.

Best bait for wrecks and artificial reefs depends on the seasons, and what each captain is looking for. Young prefers frozen Spanish sardines during fall and winter. He says the fish just stuff it right down. When live bait is available in summer, he catches them with sabiki rigs and hooks them through the tail. When these baits hit bottom, they swim straight up on

Drift fishing over deeper wrecks often means snagging wreckage, but the fish that school down there make it all worthwhile.

the leader. They look like an injured fish, and bottom predators are quick to note that. Young says pinfish are excellent in the Gulf and he used them for years around the wrecks, but he now knows how to spot sardines on the bottom in winter. They're apparently there all year long, if the winter isn't too harsh, even in water temperatures in the 50s. He says they get out in the sand, where a passing boat might not recognize them on a color bottom machine. He says in some places baitfish are there consistently. They hug bottom, getting as far from cold surface water as they can get.

For wreck fishing, Young much prefers the 80-pound stuff. He uses 8- to 10-ounce bank sinkers, with 100-pound leader for grouper, and 10/0 hooks since these fish have a big mouth. For snapper, he drops down to a 6/0 hook. "I use the cheaper, old fashioned Eagle Claw 084 bronze hook," Young says. "If I break a fish off, the hook doesn't last long in a fish. I really don't like stainless hooks left in fish."

As for reef building, he says, "Not many people dump stuff in the Atlantic like we did in Destin for years. Those Gulf spots *really* produced. We didn't have to haul it far. We would line up ranges offshore. They were trees, towers, whatever was available. The good thing was, you had to see the beach. So you were inside of eight miles. Everything we put down caught fish. Some spots are still there. Buses and Volkswagens. They've survived hurricanes, half sunk in sand, or become attached to the rock bottom."

One of the Young family's favorite wrecks they found off the Mayport jetties in the Atlantic. It was only five miles offshore, a shrimpboat from 30 to 35 feet long. After it sank at a known position, the boat rolled across the bottom for perhaps a mile, after a nor'easter storm hit. The boat was completely wrapped up in its shrimpnets. Nobody knew where it was, after the storm moved it. "When we found it one day in August," Young recalled, "there were red snapper from 8 to 10 pounds on the surface. We didn't find it by seeing fish on the surface, we did it by watching the bottom machine while running."

If you want to learn anything offshore, develop a book of numbers with your own wrecks and reefs, you have to watch that scope. And those places are out there, just waiting for someone to find them. SB

"Those places are out there, just waiting for someone to find them." Dennis Young

CHAPTER 6

Hooking, Landing, Releasing

T hese three basics are taken for granted by many fishermen, but they're vitally important. For instance, timing is everything when setting the hook, but it's a skill one has to learn, since we generally can't see what the fish is doing. There are options on how to work the rod. As for landing fish, we try to use one that will minimize the chance for a disappointing miscue. Swinging a fish in and having it thump against the side of the boat or dock is an invitation to lose it. As for releasing fish unharmed, that requires some simple techniques.

Timing is everything when you rear back or otherwise attempt to "set the hook."

Some captains now use heavy-duty landing nets to scoop up their catch, like this fine black grouper.

Setting the Hook

Pull! Show him who's boss! Bend that rod like a banana!

1. Offshore veteran shows the proper stance while waiting for a bite. **2.** Choking up on the rod butt for a powerful swing and hookset. **3.** Jamming the rod butt into gut or hip area. **4.** Quick relief after someone slaps on a rod belt.

Setting the hook at the right moment—what a difference a second can make! Or sometimes not. One fish may hit like a runaway freight train, and all the angler has to do is hang on for dear life. A second fish may mouth the bait in a sly fashion, subtle as a cat burglar. A third could pick up the bait and move toward the angler, creating a yard or two of telltale slack line.

When you've alertly determined that a bottom fish does have your bait, it's time to "cross his eyes," "set the hook," or "pull his lips off,"

in the parlance of our times. Plant your feet firmly on deck for a moment, and watch the rodtip closely. Ignore the peck-pecks of small fish, and wait for something heavier to pull the rodtip down.

When that happens, there are several options. Most people yank the rodtip skyward, cranking the reel fast enough to put a healthy bend in the rod.

See DVD for more on proper hook setting techniques.

THE "NO-SET" APPROACH

Where underwater ledges are taller and deeper, many savvy grouper diggers refrain from a "cross his eyes" hookset. In most cases there's just too much water and line stretch between you and the fish to be effective. The "no-set" approach is self-explanatory. Simply point the rod skyward, plant the rod butt in a convenient spot around the gut, and crank the reel hard for the first 20 seconds or so, keeping the rod pointed almost straight up. To avoid belly bruises, a variety of rod belts are available. Metal-tipped rod butts are discouraged here; bruises or a cracked rib are a distinct possibility. But then, grouper digging was never easy, nor for the faint of heart.

Newcomers to this sort of fishing often only hang on when a big bottom fish lunges down. It's almost as if the angler is paralyzed, incapable of using his arm muscles to lift. The rodtip is somewhere down near the water (if

Angler leans back and cranks fast to set the hook, keeping the rodtip high the entire time.

That fish has to be moved 10 feet off bottom, and right now! This technique is known as "grouper digging," and it can be brutal work. Yells of encouragement are often heaped on the lucky angler, such as: "Pull! Show him who's boss! Bend that rod like a banana!" A veteran angler will pull the rodtip high and, when he lowers the rod back down, swiftly reel in available line in a smooth and even motion.

There are two ways to bend a rod double: by reeling fast and pointing it skyward. Often it requires both. With any luck the angler responds in a vigorous fashion and the fight will soon be won. Grouper and some of the snappers will do their best to burrow under rocks or wreckage, when given half a chance. Without some hard pulling and fast reeling, these fish may reach shelter, followed by groans or curses floating on the salty air.

not underwater), the fish surging, even pulling line off the reel. The rod must be lifted skyward, and the fish turned around. There's only one way to do that, by pulling up hard and then cranking the reel fast, and preferably both at the same time. It's a game of skill with the rod, cranking the reel fast, coordinating the rod's drop with the reel's speed, a smooth effort that keeps up the pressure, and doesn't give the fish time to turn his head back around. SB

Playing and Landing Fish

Sometimes you just have to plant your feet, and do the best you can. An alert angler can even tell by the sudden squeaking of feet on a wet deck, that a good fish is hooked up. If you do get the fish a dozen feet off bottom, with good, heavy tackle, there's a 90 percent chance it won't reach bottom again. When you feel comfortable

Pull hard, then ease up after the fish is 20 feet above bottom.

with that, ease up on the pressure. Your hook may be hanging by a thread, and there's no need to rip it loose for no reason. With heav-

ier tackle, loosen the reel's drag when the fish is about 20 feet off bottom, unless you've got some giant fish with lots of fight left in him. With others, bring the fish up more gently, as it will be inflating from the pressure change, the gas inside the fish doubling every 33 feet. Gentle pumping and reeling will bring it to the surface.

In shallower water, or if the fish was hooked somewhere near the surface, grouper or snapper may continue to fight near the boat, but generally not for long. Most of their energy is expended near bottom.

Many captains in smaller boats now refrain from gaffing a nice grouper or snapper. There's no need to damage prime fish fillets. If the sides

Angler lip-gaffs a nice red snapper with a thin, stick gaff. Slamming a large gaff into the middle of a tasty bottom fish is seldom necessary, and often wastes a valuable fillet. Many of these fish are now lifted aboard simply by grabbing the leader or jig. Only the partyboats require a long, heavy gaff, since their fish have to be lifted 8 to 10 feet above the water.

of the boat are low enough, and the hook is lodged into a solid piece of lip, one can simply reach down, grab the heavy leader, and lift the fish aboard. If a jig was used, all the better—the lead makes a good handle for grabbing, between thumb and forefinger. Make sure the fish isn't thrashing on the surface, to avoid getting cut by something sharp. And never grab a trolling plug armed with treble hooks, to lift a fish aboard. Grab the leader three feet above the fish, and swing it into a fish box. If the fish is thrashing around with treble hooks, leave it alone until it quiets down. It's worth it, even if it means cutting the line and allowing the fish to sulk in the box with the leader and lucky plug. These fish, after landing on deck, can

whip a loose treble hook into a slow hand, quicker than the eye can follow. Removing a huge treble hook from an angler's hand may require the skills of a doctor back in port. Down in the Keys, in Marathon, they don't call it Fisherman's Hospital for nothing.

As for safely gaffing fish, it's customary aboard the partyboats. They fish from a deck high above water, and long gaffs are crucial. You wouldn't want to lift a 10-pound snapper 10 feet off the water, hand-lining it up. A sudden toss of its head may be enough force to pop the line or straighten the hook. You can count on a deckhand showing up with a gaff on the partyboats. It's their job. If he's skilled with the long hook, he'll nail that fish in the head.

Releasing Your Catch

Many of these fish may even require deflation, before returning to the water. They are tomorrow's catch.

Undersized snapper and grouper certainly deserve some care.

So, you've landed a grouper or snapper, and prefer to release it. With tight bag and size limits, you may have no choice. Perhaps you've already caught a limit of snapper, and were hoping for an amberjack. Or that red grouper is an inch short. There might even be a closure on Gulf red snapper that month. Or the gags may be biting so wonderfully fast, everyone on the boat has limited out.

Whatever the reason, when it's time to release a fish, be sure to do it properly. That fish represents the future.

Lay it gently on the deck, and quickly work the hook out. Hopefully, it hasn't been swallowed. Keep a pair of "hookouts" or long needlenose pliers handy, perhaps on your belt. If the hook is swallowed, it's best to cut the leader flush with the fish's lip. If using a jig, it should be easy to work loose, again using the lead head as a grip. Circle hooks are preferable because they're seldom swallowed; they pop loose rather easily with a good twist.

In many cases, a deflating tool made from stainless steel tubing may be necessary to deflate the fish. In 30 or 40 feet of water or less, this isn't necessary. But as the water gets deeper, this practice becomes increasingly necessary. The tool is inserted into the fish's side where the tip of the pectoral fin lays down against the skin. Insert the tool between scales, only an inch or two, at a 45 degree angle toward the head. You'll hear air escape from the air bladder and it will noticeably deflate if you've hit the right spot. The fish may quickly show more signs of life. Drop the fish overboard head-first, and it should swim down. It's best if the operation takes under 30 seconds.

One word of caution: some marine biologists feel that anglers should never puncture the fish's stomach, which may be protruding from its mouth. (The deeper the water, the more often that stomach will be visible.) Puncturing the thin stomach membrane while outside the fish causes problems later that are similar to a perforated stomach ulcer in people. It may be fatal to fish.

Some very conservation-minded bottom fishermen in other countries care enough about their bottom fish stocks, that they pin the fish (by the lip) to a weight with a cord attached, and drop it overboard. The fish sails back down to the bottom, where the water pressure returns the fish to its normal state—and without a puncture hole in its side. A yank pops the barb-

See DVD for more on venting and releasing fish.

less hook from its lip, and the weight is then retrieved. The fish is left on bottom, having expended no energy to get there. This fast ride back to the bottom may prevent it from being attacked by midwater barracuda, which often prey on released fish.

With that said, however, deflating and releasing snapper and grouper certainly works. A gung-ho group of fishermen on a Gulf party-boat set out to prove that point, catching and releasing 72 red snapper, a small warsaw grouper and one amberjack in 115 feet of water. Most fish were 15 to 18 inches long. Each fish was deflated, and a small spaghetti tag with a number was attached to the shoulder. The fish were tossed overboard, where 12 of them floated away belly-up on the fairly strong current. The remainder swam back down and were assumed to survive.

An hour later, scuba divers were sent down. Six tagged snapper and the grouper were observed swimming on bottom, below a layer of 15-pound amberjack hovering at mid-depth. The tagged AJ also cruised near bottom.

That was in October. The following April, six months later, a commercial boat visited the site and caught 15 of the tagged snapper and

Proper place to insert venting tool at 45 degree angle.

the warsaw on the same *day*. Two of the snapper recaptured were among 12 "floaters" that had been written off. So, releasing bottom fish in that depth (or shallower) certainly works if done properly. In cooler weather when mid-water predators such as kingfish, barracuda and amberjack have migrated south, the snappers' survival chances probably increase even more.

Research on Releasing Fish

Florida's Division of Marine Fisheries, within the Fish and Wildlife Conservation Commission (FWC), conducted studies on released fish, including grouper and snapper. Both were found to be good subjects for catch and release, with the most critical factor being the depth of water. Gentle handling, hook removal and deflation of air bladders were important.

FACTS AND FIGURES:

> Some 91 percent of red and gag grouper survived, when caught at one site in about 132 feet of water in the Gulf.

> Gag and scamp taken in 162 to 225 feet of water had only 25 and 38 percent survival rates, respectively. None of the red grouper taken in these depths survived.

> Red snapper caught in deeper waters of the Gulf also had lower survival rates. Those caught in 63 to 72 feet of water had a 99 percent survival; snappers caught in 81 to 90 feet had a 90 percent survival; and those caught in 110 to 120 feet had a 56 percent survival. Biologists felt that it made no difference in survival rates if these fish had their "everted" stomachs vented, or not.

> In another offshore study, 67 percent of vermilion snapper that were caught in 81 to 90 feet off Jacksonville survived beyond 15 days. SB

CHAPTER 7

Tackle

T ishing tackle is available in many forms, and we've tried to wade through a sea of options here, and present some clear choices often used by experienced fishermen. We've covered the gamut from baitcasting, levelwinds, spin, heavier boat rods, serious deep-drop gear, even funky sabiki rods. All have their uses at the right place and time.

Many of the wise captains carry a mix of tackle, since one never knows what sort of fish will appear during the course of a day. Light tackle may prevail over heavy, or vice versa. Newer gear may be high-tech and expensive; while older gear is legendary and still works just fine.

There is certain tackle you often see with the offshore crowd, folks who can't get enough of catching snapper and grouper.

Rack of spinning rods in the Florida Keys, ready for mangrove and yellowtail snapper. Capt. George Mitchell is up on tbe bow with his cast-net, looking for live bait.

Tackle Choices Big and Small

There are no set rules on rod and reel tackle for catching grouper and snapper. The cheapest of gear will catch Florida's mangrove snapper from bridges and piers, for instance. Drive across any bridge in the Florida Keys, or down a popular pier lined with fisher-

Angler leans back into a good fish. This boat is equipped with a variety of tackle.

men, and you see all sorts of tackle, perhaps going back several generations. Having said that, there *is* certain tackle you see more often with the offshore crowd who can't get enough of catching snapper and grouper.

Walk a crowded charterboat dock in the

Gulf or South Atlantic states, and notice what the captains use: gear they depend on for durability, dependability, reasonable cost, even salt resistance. Many offshore reels they use are referred to as 4/0 (four-ought) reels, a size determination used less and less these days. They seldom have a levelwind to feed the line evenly onto the spool. Reels without a levelwind have one less thing that can break. And fast-running offshore fish can have a detrimental effect on levelwind winds. A large capacity spool with lots of line, and no levelwind, is the preferred reel for rugged bottom fishing. The 4/0s aren't the biggest of these reels, but they're the fleet's workhorse for offshore work. And they're big enough to hold sufficient 60- or even 80-pound line to fish several hundred feet down. The majority also have a star drag, which in some situations is preferable over a lever drag. The star will screw down tight, and is just simpler to use. With a star drag reel, the drag is separate from the line release switch. A lever drag means constantly adjusting the drag lever to release line.

A two-speed reel is also an option; they can be set to retrieve line very rapidly, which serves to set the hook in deeper water. Many skippers today refrain from yanking on the line, preferring to reel rapidly instead, taking up slack, letting circle hooks or very sharp J-hooks set themselves. On the lower reel setting, a big and stubborn fish can be pulled up steadily like winching a boat onto a trailer.

For years, sturdy Penn 4/0 Senator reels were a mainstay with offshore fishermen.

See DVD for more on tackle with Rick Ryals.

Tackle for catching trophy bottom fish has come a long way since the old days. High-end, machined aluminum reels with advanced drag systems are available from many companies.

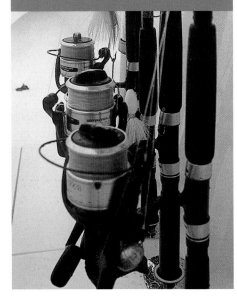

Gag grouper are capable of destroying heavier rods, when the reel's drag is locked down too tight. Sometimes lighter spin may work better.

these reels, usually six or seven feet long, and difficult to bend. You don't want a pool cue of a rod, but you certainly don't want one that bends easily. It takes muscle to move a big bottom fish toward the surface, so pick a rod that is light enough to carry all day, but strong enough to pull a grouper from his lair.

Rods with roller guides are most popular where lighter line is used. Down in the Keys, they prefer 30-pound braided line with roller guide rods. In North Florida, heavy line and standard rod guides are the norm.

Another offshore option is to carry along a longer rod, capable of lobbing a bait away from the boat, getting away from all of those vertical lines under the boat, with baits and weights lowered straight down. A single bait lobbed out into the current by itself will draw attention from roaming big snappers at mid-depth. (Not to mention passing kingfish, cobia and amberjack). One of these rods on a crowded partyboat can catch a variety of big fish that other anglers don't have a shot at.

A classic example is the fiberglass, 8-foot rods formerly made by Magna-Flex in Miami. They were often referred to as Hurricane rods, and were very durable. With 40-pound line, they could swing 12-pound amberjack over the rail of a partyboat, without benefit of a gaff. Using a levelwind reel, that combo could lob a 3-ounce lead jig away from the boat and plumb the depths. Same with a large menhaden bait. Levelwinds tend to wear out after countless battles on 40-pound line, which is hard work on the gears. The Shimano 15 reel with a tougher lever drag can be used, but it takes a careful thumb and some practice to prevent untimely backlashes. Both outfits can really lean on big fish hard enough to land them on crowded partyboats. (Some partyboat captains now frown on long casts, because of possible injury to nearby anglers.)

Tossing out baits and jigs with a big spinning rod is easier, even with underhand casts. The problem is that spin is less efficient in

Many survive today, workable reels that are prized and sought on the Internet, sold on E-Bay. A newer model has replaced the old, and you see them on many charterboats.

Workhorse reels commonly favored by the fleet include the Penn 113H, Penn HLW Wide, Daiwa 400 Sealine and the Daiwa 350H. Shimano, Shakespeare, Okuma, Quantum and other companies produce quality reels of similar size.

A wide variety of rod brands compliment

pressuring big fish away from other anglers' lines. On smaller boats, the combination of open water and elbow room means spin tackle is more practical, if big fish don't have to be manhandled out of a solid rockpile or wreck.

Spin gear does, however, work great at jigging up some surprisingly big bottom fish. Some catches seem impossible on this gear, hard evidence that bottom fish wander far from cover, too far to return. It's only a matter of time before they can be cranked up. Stronger spin tackle is also good at drift-fishing, dropping egg weights and whole baits down to 200 feet. Again, bottom predators follow the drifting boat, grab the bait, and under pressure, can't seem to find their way back to safe cover.

This same gear with 25-pound line has a surprising level of success in veteran hands, pulling out gag grouper while the boat is anchored over rocks. With a medium-action rod of eight feet, one can entice wary gags into biting, long after they've stopped hitting heavier, 50-pound outfits. Toss a live pinfish behind the boat with a 2-ounce egg sinker, and a slim 40-pound leader, and watch who gets the strike. It requires hard pulling to coax them up, however, when the boat is anchored so close to heavy grouper cover.

One will also find useful workhorses in the field of bait-

casting gear—sort of beefed-up versions of traditional bass tackle. Pack one of these reels with 20- or 25-pound line, and they're capable of landing 20-pound snapper and grouper, when used in capable hands. An Ambassador 6500 reel or one of its cousins, lobbing jigs or baits off the stern of a partyboat, is capable of winning the fish pot for big snapper.

Even light spin tackle with 12- to 15-pound line will catch a variety of snapper and grouper.

Two captains gearing up for Keys reef fishing trip.

Sabiki Rods

Odd-looking sabiki rods were developed for fishermen who insist on using live bait most of the time, utilizing those efficient, 6-hook sabiki bait rigs.

The tiny multi-hook sabiki flies seem to snag in everything, including people, though tiny hooks are fairly easy to remove. Anglers using spin or heavier gear are used to having their sabiki rigs poking into various items, but they get used to it. Or they learn to hook each pair of hooks together and wrap the entire affair around the rod itself, when the day is done.

For those who prefer something more efficient, there is always the "sabiki rod," made by various companies listed on Internet search engines. These are hollow, plastic tubes that allow the entire hook rig to be reeled up inside the rod, without snagging even the rod tip, whose plastic lip is wider than the hooks. Most levelwind reels will easily attach to these rods. When enough bait is caught, the sabiki rod is stored like any other, but without the exposed hooks. SB

Heavier reels on boat rods come in two flavors: those with a star drag like the one at left, and the lever drag on the right. Grouper fishermen who use the tightest drags possible generally prefer the star drag.

Baitcasting gear with a levelwind reel, or spin gear, is advisable for jigging up bottom fish.

These fish are sometimes caught in open channels or anywhere with hard, flat, rock bottom, and there is no urgency to horse them away from anything. They may run like a redfish across the open, sand bottom, hunting for cover. In this way, gags up to 26 inches have been landed on 10-pound spin by the editor.

GARY FOLDEN

The typical grouper rod is six to seven feet long and should be very firm in flex. (The old-timers would find something stout as a pool cue.) The rod should be able to bend a little with a big fish, however. There is a tremendous amount of pressure applied to the rod during the fight, so strong, quality-built rod guides are a must.

used for grouper fishing. The size of the reel should match the depth of water. Unlike the speedy king mackerel, grouper seldom run more than 30 feet. The reel's drag must be capable of tightening down to a point where no line can escape. Some fishermen lock the drag down with pliers to ensure no slippage. I prefer to hand tighten the drag, so under the most extreme cases (200-pound goliath grouper) the drag will grudgingly give up line. One veteran angler out of Suwannee was almost pulled overboard when a 40-pound

These anglers happily hooked into some big grouper. They were both using heavier boat rods.

When fishing in 40 or 50 feet, I like to set the hook by yanking straight up on the rod and let the fish fight the bend in the rod, while I attempt to turn the handle on the reel. In deep water, it's best to just start cranking fast and hard. This method will take up stretch in the line better and prevents getting "rocked-up."

Conventional or baitcasting reels are much preferred over spin tackle. These reels are better suited to handle heavier lines generally

kingfish grabbed his grouper bait on the bottom. He had screwed down his reel's drag on the 80-pound line a bit too tight. One never knows what may bite on the bottom, so it's wise to give up line when called for.

Reels that have a low gear ratio are preferable to high-speed reels in shallower water. The lower speed provides more torque, so the angler can crank the handle more easily. Grouper tackle is not particularly suitable for other types of fishing, except perhaps for red snapper in deeper water. This tackle is pretty much limited to bottom fishing. The Penn 4/0 was the standard grouper reel for many years. Other brands of that size and stature have since appeared on the market, such as the Daiwa Sealine and slightly smaller Pflueger Contender.

Captain's Choice   Gary Folden

"Some anglers lock the drag down to ensure no slippage."

Elated angler cranked up this scamp grouper.

> **Daiwa Sealine reels**

> **Penn 113H reels**

> **Not much spinning gear**

RICK RYALS

For most of my life, I've used the heaviest tackle I could find to fish grouper. Tough, 100-pound line and leader used to be my standard. I'm a big fan of Penn 113Hs, and Daiwa 400Hs on a solid glass, 50-pound class rod. However, over the years, I've begun to realize the fun and deadly effectiveness of lighter tackle. While it's true a gag will immediately head for cover when he feels the hook, I've learned that 30-pound mono spooled on a kingfish-style conventional reel, on a soft tip glass rod, often won't panic him until it's too late. I don't know how many times we've hooked a nice gag on 20- to 30-pound tackle, and just

Capt. Gary Folden's boat returns at sunset after a long day off-shore, fishing grouper rocks.

had him run around a little.

Each angler on the boat needs to start with a 4/0 reel loaded with 50-pound test, mounted on a stout 40-pound class rod. That's perfect for dropping baits down in a heavy current, or while making a fast drift. Or if gag grouper are present and prove too strong for lighter gear. Each angler also needs a high-speed 20-pound

class reel loaded with 30-pound test, and a corresponding light glass rod, for use after anchoring. I've had much better luck on mono than I've had with braided line. Granted, braided is stronger for its diameter, has greater sensitivity, and one can fish it with very little weight. However, I feel like we lose a lot more fish because it won't stretch when a

Captain's Choice Rick Ryals

See DVD for more on Rick Ryals' top picks.

big snapper bucks his head. I use braid for vermilion snapper, triggerfish and sometimes grouper. But not for big red snapper.

Popular reels include the Penn 113H and Penn HLW Wide. Also the Daiwa 440 Sealine for heavier line and the Daiwa 350H for 30- or 40-pound line. Lighter gear would include such reels as the Ambassadeur 6500, Shimano Speedmaster, the Penn 545, Calcutta 700 and Pflueger Contender.

GEORGE MITCHELL

For catching yellowtails on the reefs, most anglers in the Keys prefer spinning gear in the 10- to 20-pound range. I prefer a Penn 560 Slammer spinning reel for two reasons: It has a

"I feel like we lose more fish because braided line won't stretch when a big snapper bucks his head."

> Heavier 4/0 class reels and rods, including Penn 113H and HLW Wides, and Daiwa 440 Sealines.

> Lighter gear is matching rods with Ambassadeur 6500, Shimano Speedmaster, Penn 545, Calcutta 700 and Pflueger Contender.

Rick Ryals' gear is no-nonsense, heavier bottom fishing gear, with line ranging from 30- to 80-pound.

super-consistent drag and holds plenty of 15-pound line. Sometimes the fish are way back behind the boat, and a smaller spool might be almost empty before even reaching the fish. Hook into something big back there with a near-empty spool, and the fight won't last 10 seconds. If a reel is "spooled" or emptied by a big fish, it pays to keep an extra spool of line handy for the same reel. Make it the same class of line, or one step heavier. And, no matter what reel you use, it's very important to use clear line. Our yellowtail snapper live in clear water and can be line-shy.

You should also have a bigger rod ready, perhaps a 4/0 outfit, because sooner or later someone is going to yell, "Holy cow, there's a 20-pound grouper down there!"

It also pays to have a 20-pound spinning rod set up with 30-pound mono line. Rig it to a wire leader with a stinger hook. It isn't always barracuda that steal half of your yellowtails...we've caught our fair share of whopper kingfish and a few wahoo, while anchored and chumming for yellowtails.

I spend most of my time anchored a little ways offshore, so our gear is a little stronger than bridge fishermen use. Out there, you never know when some late-night 6-pound

Florida Keys boats carry light spin for yellowtail snapper.

Captain's Choice

"I spend most of my time anchored offshore, so our gear is a little stronger than bridge fishermen use. Out there, you never know when some late-night 6-pound mangrove snapper will try to burrow under a rock."

> 15-pound spin gear.

> Heavier spin with 20- to 30-pound line.

> Standard 4/0 bottom outfits 50-pound line.

mangrove snapper will try to burrow under a rock. My inshore gear consists of stout, 15- to 20-pound spinning outfits loaded with clear 20-pound Ande line.

Deepwater tackle should be a little more stout, since bigger mangroves are mostly caught offshore. I prefer my 20-pound sailfish spinning rods, again using the clear line.

One exception is the heavier bottom rod, which we use in the spread. This is a 30-pound conventional outfit with a longer 50-pound leader.

Tackle for mutton snapper varies depending on the situation but as a rule, nothing less than 20-pound gear should even be considered. I like a medium to heavy, 6 ½-foot conventional rod with a two-speed 30 reel. The longer stick gives you plenty of upward sweep as you pump that fish to the surface, and the two-speed reel helps if you encounter a whopper mutton or a really nice grouper.

George Mitchell's boat bristles with an assortment of rod outfits and rod holders.

Twelve-volt Kristal Reel loaded with several thousand feet of braided line, ready to drop seven baits. Note the attached light.

Deep Drop Tackle

For tackle, almost anything in the 50-pound class or higher will get baits to the bottom. Getting it back, preferably with fish, is the problem. The most popular deep-drop reel is the Kristal, which has a self-contained, strong motor that is watertight, pulls hard, and with a reasonable price. They also run on 12 volts, so that's good for recreational users. "Mine is set up for a bent butt rod, a short rod that stays in the rod holder," says Capt. George LaBonte. "The reel is a little heavy, but could work in a standup harness if the angler wants to stand up. There is also the Lindgren-Pittman tackle, which is the commercial industry standard. It runs on 24 volts. Many of the billfish boats in The Bahamas now have one, hooked up to an 80- or 130-pound, bent butt rod.

There is also Electra-Mate, which makes an electric reel that will mount on a rod. If the electrics go out, you can manually retrieve the fish. With the other outfits, if they lose electric power, you have to hand-line the fish up."

Super Lines

The accepted line for deep-drop reels are the "super lines," made from Spectra fiber. These are very thin, braided polyethylene lines. Depending on the reel size, anglers are spooling up with 80- to 200-pound test. Many anglers buy a thousand yards of the stuff, which costs about $150. It's so thin, some reels will hold about a mile of it, which is impractical and expensive. So, most reels have cheap, old-fashioned Dacron line as backing, with at least a thousand feet of super line tied over that. Like Dacron, the super lines have no stretch, and you can feel every bite down there, giving an indication when it's time to reel up. Simple Dacron has been used in a thousand feet of water, but it's fatter and the current pulls on it much more. Same with monofilament line, though it stretches so much, you literally can't feel the fight from a 50-pound grouper. SB

At top, Kristal 12-volt outfit. Also above, Lindgren-Pittman reel runs on 24 volts and attaches to bent-butt rods. Right, Electra-Mate attaches to standard partyboat tackle.

CHAPTER 8

Bottom
Rigs

Things can get complicated with bottom fishing gear for snapper and grouper. There are many more styles of hooks, even in color. Leader lengths and styles have multiplied. Bank and egg sinkers have stayed the same; both were time-tested for many years. Two-way swivels are much darker to avoid mackerel cutoffs, while three-way swivels haven't changed. Jigs with feathery or twister worm tails, or sweetened with various natural baits, are still highly effective. The newer jigging spoons painted in baitfish patterns, some re-rigged with a single hook, also work well.

In the old days you were handed a *very* sturdy rod with two or three hooks...

 See DVD for more bottom rigs.

A wide variety of tackle will catch snapper and grouper. Gag grouper at right was taken with old but reliable sliding egg sinker rig.

Choosing the Right Rigs

For more than a century, bottom rigs for snapper and grouper consisted of two or three J-hooks or circle hooks, rigged on small drops just above a "bank sinker" of 12 or 16 ounces. These simple rigs caught millions of pounds of snapper and grouper. If you fished on a partyboat or charterboat, you were handed a sturdy rod with two or three of these hooks, and told to cut bait. Lots of bait. That simple bottom rig caught snapper from eight inches long, on up to 25 pounds or so. Not that many big fish, on the average, unless they were really biting that day.

Those "chicken" or "guppy rigs" earned the nickname in later years, because they caught so many small snapper. They were effective and identical to commercial fishing gear and still work today, but the problem is they catch too many small bottom fish that represent the fishery's future. Even when properly deflated and released, snapper and grouper can still be seized by bigger predators on the surface or at mid-depth, before reaching comparative safety on the bottom. Releasing small fish all day while hoping for bigger ones is hard on the resource. This small fish rig also isn't ideal for luring bigger fish, though admittedly they do work at times.

Before bag and size limits, the chicken rigs were practical for catching a variety of bottom fish. One could crank up several snapper and white trout at the same time. Or a combination of triggerfish, grouper and amberjack. Pulling up a string of unknown fish can be comparable to lifting a heavy weight, but there is some excitement and speculation in what might be brought up. And big fish do live on the bottom. The editor's biggest red snapper for many years was a 25-pounder that ate the head from a 3-pound spotted seatrout. It grabbed his bottom circle hook on a wintry day in January.

Today, with strict bag and size limits (not to mention closed seasons on red snapper in the Gulf), wise anglers are using more selective gear. Whether the bag limit for red snapper is two or five, anglers are aiming for quality. For instance, many now realize that an egg weight with a single, large bait like a Spanish sardine or cigar minnow will invariably catch bigger bot-

With strict bag and size limits, wise anglers are using more selective bottom gear.

Fish hugger with a fine doubleheader of red grouper caught with cut bait.

tom fish that are suspended above bottom. Even a 2-ounce bucktail jig, sweetened with an entire cigar minnow, will catch double-digit snapper all day when they're feeding at mid-depth. This can be done with repeated drifts through the strike zone, or by anchoring and casting.

The sliding egg is by far the most popular saltwater bottom rig in shallow water, but it works very well offshore with sufficient lead. It's usually rigged with about 30 inches of mono leader, with a small, black barrel swivel separat-

Above, sliding egg. Below, double swivel sinker.

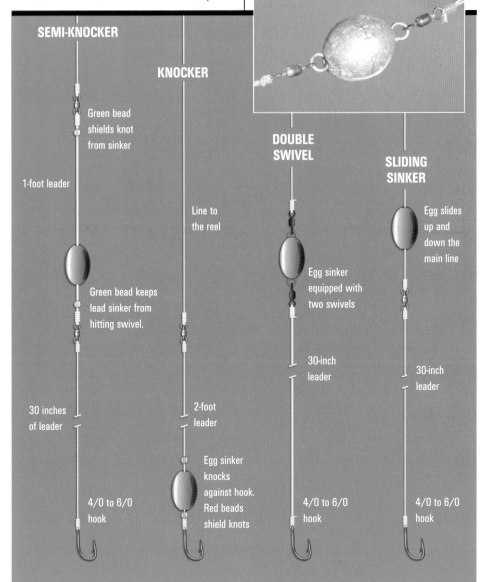

SEMI-KNOCKER

Green bead shields knot from sinker

1-foot leader

Green bead keeps lead sinker from hitting swivel.

30 inches of leader

4/0 to 6/0 hook

KNOCKER

Line to the reel

2-foot leader

Egg sinker knocks against hook. Red beads shield knots

4/0 to 6/0 hook

DOUBLE SWIVEL

Egg sinker equipped with two swivels

30-inch leader

4/0 to 6/0 hook

SLIDING SINKER

Egg slides up and down the main line

30-inch leader

4/0 to 6/0 hook

SLIDER AND KNOCKER BASICS

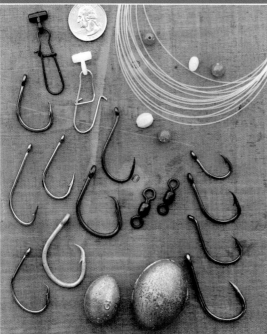

Knocker rigs are used with live baits that are strong enough to pull hard.

against the hook itself. This is used almost strictly with a live bait that is strong enough, when hooked through the tail, to swim several feet away from the weight. Veteran anglers with a sure touch and a keen eye can set the hook apparently while the bottom fish is still tugging, before it pulls the short leader entirely through the egg weight, hitting the swivel. This rig is much better for lobbing, since the egg weight can't wander far from the hook. (Casting and having a sliding egg weight land 20 feet from the bait can be tiresome, especially when seabirds are diving after your bait, which is sinking far too slowly without the attendant lead). As a reminder, tackle stores often carry small, plastic beads that should ride on either side of the lead weight. In a sudden battle the lead may slam into the hook's knot, weakening it. The bead lessens that impact.

With the semi-knocker rig, the egg sinker still slides up and down, but is confined between two small, black swivels perhaps two feet apart. This method also requires plastic beads to lessen shock and stress on the knots. The 2-foot leader also makes for a short reaction time before the fish begins dragging the weight. With a relatively smart mangrove snapper, knocker rigs may spook the fish when it feels weight behind it, and the angler may not have time to react. A grouper or amberjack might not care, however. Both knocker rigs keep the leader on a very short leash compared with the sliding egg, where a snapper could bolt with the bait 10 feet without dragging or feeling that egg weight.

ing leader and line. Since the weight slides up and down the main line, a discerning bottom fish feels little or no resistance, as it makes off with the bait. In reality, an alert angler will feel the fish pull the rodtip down. The angler responds with a sharp yank, and the battle is on. Countless people have used this rig, and that's why Florida tackle stores are well-stocked with egg weights of many sizes. For catching the sly mangrove snapper, this rig has never really been improved upon through the years, though there have been modifications.

For bottom fishing in, say, 60 to 80 feet, the knocker rig is an egg weight that slaps up

SMALL IS BETTER FOR YELLOWTAIL

Small hooks and tiny weights are a hallmark of yellowtail fishing. Baits are almost floated back in the current, with just enough lead to stay several feet below the surface. Yellowtail rise up in the chumline and grab anything drifting with the current in a natural fashion.

For bigger fish, a pair of hooks can be used on the leader, rigged about five inches apart, with the back hook as a "stinger" for short strikes. A favorite hook for this in South Florida is Mustad's 39950, a strong, bronze hook with a slight offset. A live bait can be pinned at both ends, and lowered down on a 4-foot leader, with enough egg weight to reach bottom. The leader is usu- ally 80-pound monofilament or fluorocarbon. It's a great rig for big mutton snapper and black grouper, but has applications for other bottom fish. A big red snapper would certainly grab it. The rig can be lowered down to about 200 feet with a big enough sliding egg weight.

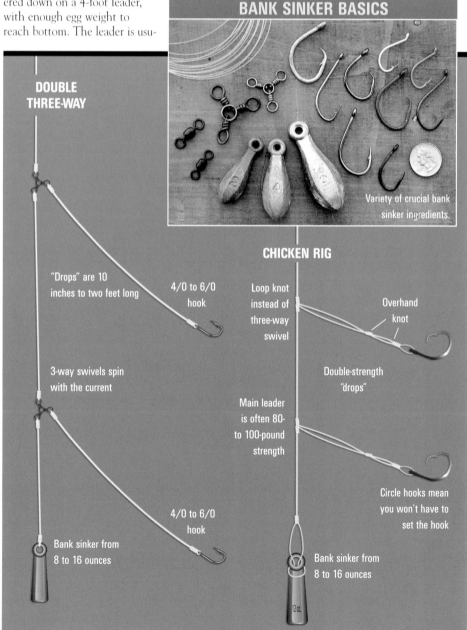

BANK SINKER BASICS

Variety of crucial bank sinker ingredients.

DOUBLE THREE-WAY

"Drops" are 10 inches to two feet long

4/0 to 6/0 hook

3-way swivels spin with the current

4/0 to 6/0 hook

Bank sinker from 8 to 16 ounces

CHICKEN RIG

Loop knot instead of three-way swivel

Overhand knot

Double-strength "drops"

Main leader is often 80- to 100-pound strength

Circle hooks mean you won't have to set the hook

Bank sinker from 8 to 16 ounces

The first hook is buried in the bait's front end, so that it moves through the water in a streamlined fashion.

Another interesting bottom rig, more popular in South Florida where you're fishing in deeper water with strong currents, is what we'll

Above, heavy jigging spoons. Some are re-rigged with single hooks. Below, red grouper on circle hook. Right, vermilion snapper on double bottom rig.

call the three-way rig. This entails using a bank sinker of varying weight, just big enough to hit bottom promptly and under the boat. The familiar, 3-way swivel is three feet above the lead.

The unusual part is a leader of about 14 feet, also tied to the swivel. When the weight hits bottom, the bait is 14 feet away, slowly falling the remaining distance, like a free piece of chum—or, if a live bait, free to run around on a long leash in a natural fashion. It appears to have no attachments, except for a strong little bronze hook that is hard to see. Even the smartest mutton snapper in blue water has a difficult time ignoring something so appealing. As for grouper, the sight of a frantic baitfish (like a strong little blue runner) running around on a long leader is enough to incite a riot.

The downside to this arrangement is that it's difficult to feel a bite. Often, the fish swallows the hook. And, when the swivel is reeled to

boatside, the angler must grab the 14-foot leader and hand-line the fish the rest of the way. While many anglers are new to hand-lining fish, it does carry some excitement. And it lands some tremendous mutton snapper down in South Florida.

The single dropper rig is built for strength and targeting big fish. Anglers who want big snapper and grouper in several hundred feet of water grab a length of 150-pound mono leader, and tie a 16-ounce weight on the end. Three feet above the lead, they gather a loop of leader, creating a loop two feet in diameter. Tie three overhand knots in the loop (a surgeon's knot) and slowly pull the loop tight. One can put the loop under a shoe, and pull the knot tight by tugging upwards on line and sinker. Next, clip the loop in one spot only an inch from the knot. This suddenly creates a 4-foot length of leader, and the hook is attached to the end. A strong, black swivel is attached several feet up the leader above the knot. The bait is usually a whole cigar minnow, or perhaps a sturdy belly strip from a bonito or a live blue runner. A circle hook can be used if grouper are around, which means the angler won't have to set the hook. Or something very similar, like the Mustad 10827BLN. If the fish are picky and smart like big snapper, then a sharp J-hook may be used—though the angler will have to reel furiously to tighten the line up if it's monofilament. (Another favorite for South Florida anglers, who use smaller live pilchards for this work, is the bronze Mustad 92677 hook, with a big offset.)

The sliding swivel rig is another innovation. This requires a 2-foot leader connecting a bank sinker to a strong, black swivel, which slides on the main line above the swivel connecting to the leader. What is different is that another black swivel is free to slide up and down. Attached to swivel number two is a dozen feet of fluorocarbon or mono leader, with another dark hook at the end. This sliding swivel is more stealthy than using a gold, 3-way swivel, and the live bait is free to run around the sinker with no twisting of the line.

Bottom hooks have progressed a long way since a few years ago, and some today are razor sharp. One favorite is the Owner SSW Live Bait hook, in size 6/0. Others are chemically sharpened and given the name of Lazer.

Popular hooks today are thick and strong, rather short-shanked, and either black or bronze. Whether one buys expensive hooks or cheap, using sharp hooks is imperative. There are missed strikes on every trip offshore, often from the biggest fish of the day. A dull hook may ricochet from a grouper's mouth. Even a sharp hook can get wadded up inside the bait, while a fish thoughtfully munches it. In that event a dull hook won't even emerge from the bait, much less penetrate a tough grouper or snapper's mouth.

As for line, keep in mind there is major stretch in mono line, especially when fishing 200 feet down. This is a great application for braided line on the reel, in the 50- to 80-pound class. SB

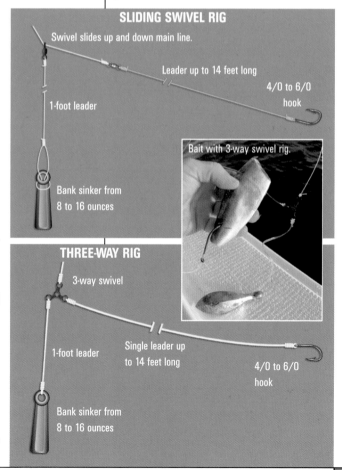

SLIDING SWIVEL RIG

Swivel slides up and down main line.

Leader up to 14 feet long

4/0 to 6/0 hook

1-foot leader

Bank sinker from 8 to 16 ounces

Bait with 3-way swivel rig.

THREE-WAY RIG

3-way swivel

1-foot leader

Single leader up to 14 feet long

4/0 to 6/0 hook

Bank sinker from 8 to 16 ounces

CHAPTER 9

Baits

Picking the right baits for an off-shore trip is something of a guessing game. There are no rules set in concrete, and the bait-catching angler willing to think outside the box may land bigger bottom fish on any given weekend. Most anglers grab a few boxes of frozen bait, or maybe a bucket of live stuff from the marina. Or they catch live baits on the water, which is always a good idea. Those that think ahead keep a couple of bait traps in the bay, sitting overnight with a block of frozen chum. Other anglers are expert with huge castnets that can cover the width of an entire bayou or marsh creek. All it takes is a little ingenuity to gain an edge over the competition.

When using any bait, be *sure* to leave the point of the hook at least partially exposed.

Spanish sardines school nervously with big predators lurking below. Below, frozen sardines being prepared for a drop on the offshore reefs. Heads and tails are removed to make "plugs."

Baits for Snapper and Grouper

Baits for snapper and grouper vary widely. Both will eat almost anything they can sink their teeth into, when they've a mind to. Or they can be finicky, forcing anglers to try a variety of baits before finding success. On the older partyboats, you were given a ladle and pointed at a washtub full of thawed, purple squid from California. Or a box or flat of menhaden, today called "pogies" or "shad." Or buckets of bycatch from a shrimp-boat, which would include all sorts of goodies such as sand trout, croakers, small flounder or small Gulf squid. Mixed with a few catfish, with their poisonous fins.

Today, many Gulf and Atlantic anglers simply buy 5-pound boxes of cigar minnows or Spanish sardines, along with squid. Some anglers catch their own live baits as insurance, since most boats today have their own livewells. Here's what our three captains had to say about bait in their local waters:

GARY FOLDEN

Bait for gag grouper could be almost anything; they have such a varied diet. Small fish are prey for gags, with squid and shrimp a popular second choice. The most available frozen baits at coastal marinas and bait camps are cigar minnows, Spanish sardines, scaled sardines and squid. These are all fine baits and can be used whole or cut into sections. If you use a whole baitfish, be sure to twist or cut the tail open. This allows scent to waft from the bait, and it certainly helps to get the bite going.

Other fish we use for grouper baits, when cut into sections, are thread herring, blue runners, grunts, pinfish, ladyfish, ballyhoo, bluefish, lizardfish, cutlassfish (ribbonfish), mullet, mackerel, menhaden, sand perch, squirrelfish, tomtate (called ruby redlips), croakers and chunks of bonito (little tunny). Most of these fish are not available at bait shops, but they can be castnetted or caught on a hook and line before or during the trip. For instance, a half-hour of casting small jigs on the summertime grassflats or channels, perhaps with a chumbag in the water, will often produce many of these same fish. If so, you'll need a cutting board to fillet them later while

Above, live shrimp ready for the hook. Below, Spanish sardines roam a livewell on their first snapper and grouper trip.

See DVD for more information on baits.

Above, cigar minnow, pilchard and Spanish sardine, just caught with sabiki rigs off Florida's east coast. Below, fresh cast-netted ballyhoo in the Upper Florida Keys, ready for bottom fishing duties. Some fine baits.

offshore. Even a small piece of plywood can serve well. It will absorb much of the mess and all of the knife scratches.

When using any bait, be sure to leave the point of the hook at least partially exposed. This allows for a more positive hookset, and results in fewer missed strikes. When using whole baits or head sections, I will either nose-hook or eye-hook the offering. Baits hooked in this fashion are more hydrodynamic and dive to the bottom quicker and with less spin.

Often, live baits will coax gag grouper to bite when a dead bait is ignored. At appropriate sizes, all of the above-mentioned species will make good live baits. One favorite is the plentiful pinfish. This prickly little fellow is hardy

Mighty Menhaden

Menhaden, nicknamed "pogies" or "shad," are the most important baitfish in the Southeastern United States. They supported a billion-pound commercial harvest each year, until their numbers declined for reasons not so mysterious. Before other baitfish species from Florida were boxed and sold to marinas from Texas to North Carolina, it was the pogy that generations of fishermen used to catch their red snapper and grouper.

In fact, prior to the 1980s, most snapper fishermen in Louisiana and Texas had never seen a box of cigar minnows or Spanish sardines as bait. They were raised using inexpensive menhaden instead. Turns out they were a pretty good bait.

Bought in hundred-pound boxes or 25-pound "flats," this bait is good insurance when running offshore, especially on overnight trips.

Menhaden are universally loved by many species of fish; they have an oily flavor with a high amount of amino acids that fish crave. The oil of menhaden is so precious, it's bottled and sold as the ultimate fish attractant.

Frozen, live, chunked, chummed or applied as two kinds of oil (emulsified or surface-floating regular), this is a valuable coastal baitfish that deserves protective regulations against overfishing. SB

and easy to keep alive in baitwells. They're cast-netted or easily hook-and-lined using small pieces of bait on hair hooks or sabiki rigs. Pinfish are very active on a hook when sent to the bottom. Their actions when a grouper appears often alert the angler, because the nervous wiggles telegraph right up the line. Another bait that wiggles even harder, because they're much stronger, are small blue runners. On a 5-foot leader on bottom, their evasive actions will elude capture for a few moments, driving grouper into a frenzy of pursuit until the runner is finally gobbled down. All of this can easily be felt on a rod and reel, 50 feet above, if the water isn't too choppy.

The small, gold or red hook bait-catching rigs commonly called "sabiki rigs" are very effective in catching myriad filter-feeding live fish, such as sardines. These rigs make acquiring an adequate supply of live bait very easy. Drop one of these six-hook (tiny fly) rigs down around an offshore buoy, channel marker or jetty, and you may have six baitfish hooked up at once. These baits are plentiful from late spring to early fall. The same rigs, each hook baited with a tiny piece of squid, are used to catch pinfish and spottail pinfish. The former prefer thick grassflats, while the latter lurk around rock patches in seven to 15 feet of water. A can of fish-flavored cat food, or red-label jack mackerel is a worthwhile investment, to shorten the time necessary to catch a trip's worth of pinfish and other baits. Mix with a little water and shake, then pour overboard.

RICK RYALS

While working on partyboats in the 1960s, one of my jobs was to cut up bonito and squid for the customers. We had no cigar minnows, or even fresh sardines. I can't believe we ever caught big snapper. But we certainly did.

Live bait is easily available when the water is warm, but in the depths of winter, I'd much rather have a big chunk of fresh bonito, or a butterflied grunt, or vermilion snapper.

We've also had great success with a dirty little trick we call a "smorgasbord." That's a huge gob of bait, consisting of a grunt's head, a couple of squid, and whatever else is left on the cutting board. Drop it to the bottom, and it will chum up every grunt or vermilion snapper in the neighborhood. The trick is to let them pick at it, until their efforts attract the attention of a big gag. When the nibbles stop, get ready.

I've caught grouper on almost every kind of

As for snapper, live bait is the key to today's fishery on the Eastern Seaboard. Thank goodness for sabiki rigs.

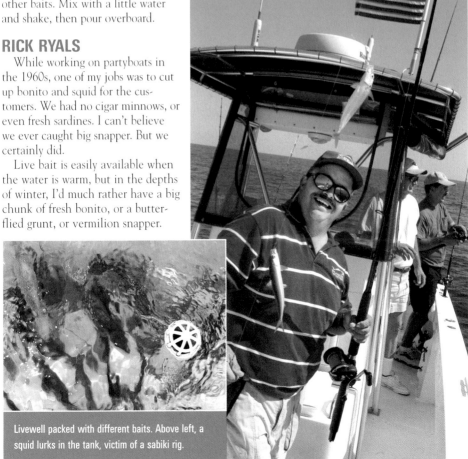

Livewell packed with different baits. Above left, a squid lurks in the tank, victim of a sabiki rig.

live bait, but there are favorites of mine that people seldom use. Gags are not so selective as snapper and they don't seem to mind sharp spines on a bait, as snapper do. If amberjack aren't chewing us up, I love a fat, frisky pinfish. Pogies (menhaden) reign supreme, and the usual cigar minnows, greenies (thread herring) and sardines caught on sabiki rigs are excellent. Over on the Gulf side, lizardfish are the best-kept secret grouper bait. Croakers are another

secret weapon. Their low-frequency croaking carries a long way underwater, a distress signal that grouper can find in the murkiest water.

As for snapper bait, live bait is the key to today's fishery: For all the advancements in bottom fishing electronics, has anything else really improved snapper fishing as much as the simple sabiki (bait-catching) rigs?

It's true that snapper eat just about anything. I've retrieved toy plastic action figures

Above, chumming ballyhoo within range of castnet on the patch reefs. Anglers even catch them with hair hooks.

from their stomachs, as well as old pop tops from beer cans. However, I would not recommend either as favorite baits. The subject of bait is a lot like discussions on the best kind of bottom. There are no rules set in concrete here. Live bait is usually best and there are plenty of days we spend as much time catching bait with sabiki rigs as we do actually fishing for bottom fish. Live cigar minnows, squid and frisky sardines work best, but they migrate far to the south in winter. If you can find grunts and pinfish in colder weather, they'll work.

It pays to experiment. For instance, if you want to see a winter snapper lose his mind, show him a jumbo live shrimp. The shrimp works all year, but it's only in the dead of winter that grunts and pinfish thin out enough to let a snapper find the shrimp. There is one more bait that anglers should never throw back. It seems that no oversized snapper will let a live sand perch hang around for long. You won't get many bites using the perch, but when you do…hang on to that rod.

In water hovering around 60 degrees or colder, everything changes. Bait becomes scarce and snapper move much slower. That's when it becomes so important to anchor before fishing. Also, remember to let your bait soak a good while on bottom, before deciding the fish won't bite. You'll probably be using either frozen cigar minnows or sardines, and remember not to defrost them. Unless you have fresh minnows (very unlikely in winter), you'll want to drop them to the bottom frozen. They stay on the hook better and bait stealers can't pick them apart. A snapper will see the little fish trying to peck at your bait, and the big guy will swallow it whole. We call frozen sardines "popsicles," and have come to rely on them, as they're much more effective

bait than the mushy, thawed-out version.

How do you keep frozen bait hard as a brick in the boat all day? We use a thermal bag available from the frozen food section at Sam's Club. Price is about six dollars.

GEORGE MITCHELL

Speaking of baits, it can get a little tricky here in South Florida. I like to bring a lot of choices, and the fresher the better. Top picks

George Mitchell waits for the right moment with his huge castnet.

are ballyhoo, mullet, pilchards, squid and silversides. The best deal is to purchase it fresh, and then package and freeze them in 1-pound bags. That way you don't defrost and ruin a lot of bait on a slow day when the fish won't eat. Yellowtail snapper here are a finicky bunch: some days they'll eat nothing but ballyhoo strips, and then squid the very next day. They might even change their minds in the middle of the bite. One good tactic is to switch baits periodically, just to see if a bigger fish grabs on.

For mangrove snapper during spring, the most popular bait will be finger mullet, which are everywhere. Your best bet is to castnet them. Keep a few dozen alive in your well, but

Pinfish live and chunked. Below, Capt. Jack Carlson empties one of his pinfish traps into the livewell before heading offshore of Marathon, Florida.

brine the rest in a bucket of salt water and ice. Brining them preserves them for use for a couple days, or for freezing.

Before you bait up, scan the bait box and figure out the best offerings you have, and start with the least popular first. We begin by tossing out a few pieces of fresh dead shrimp; that usually gets their attention. Next, you should put a hook in one, but remember, you want it to look just like the freebies, so let it drift back naturally. After they catch on to that, it's time to switch over to live shrimp. Once they learn that drill, you can switch back to cut shrimp, but better yet, try fresh mullet chunks. That should really get them going. As a last resort, you can switch over to a live finger mullet, but remember to let them run with it, before setting the hook.

For targeting mangrove snappers in the shallows other than during spring, your best baits will be shrimp and pinfish. Fish the shrimp as described above, but the pinfish will require a little surgery. I like to catch at least 30 pinfish for a mangrove outing, or 10 per angler. We don't mind if some of the baits expire after they're caught. It's best to remove them from the livewell and brine them. These can be used as "steaks."

Before steaking a pinfish, you will first need to give them a haircut. That means removing the dorsal spines and pectoral fins first. This makes the bait easier to swallow. I like to use my wife's stainless steel poultry scissors, though for some reason she doesn't really approve of this. After the haircut, steak the pinfish by angling back from the head down to the belly area. An average pinfish will yield three steaks, while a whopper may produce as many as five. Keep the baits on ice, since they deteriorate quickly. Remember to toss some freebies as chum to get the bite going, before baiting a hook.

The live "pinnies," as we call pinfish, will be saved for

bigger mangroves. I like to give these baits a dorsal haircut too. Their dorsal spines are a defensive tool used to thwart predators, so trimming them drives the snappers nuts. They become more active, and are less likely to dive into cover.

As for offshore baits, it pays to bring along the usual choices, but the best baits will be pilchards that appear in your chum slick after sunset. We begin fishing before the sun goes down, primarily to get a few yellowtails, but also to get the speedos and ballyhoo in the slick, since they make great baits also. And remember, the more chum the better. Keep the bag full and add a scoop of "slop" (home-made chum) to the menhaden oil slick every few minutes. I've had nights out there where we had nice mangroves right behind the boat, and caught limit of whoppers quickly. Other nights, the big ones won't show up until the moon pops over the horizon.

Anchor up out there at night, put in some time with these techniques, and I guarantee you'll hook into some big, fine mangroves. SB

Mutton Snapper Basics

Captain George Mitchell says that once you've settled in and the 'hoos (ballyhoo) are chummed up, it's time to deploy the baits. He usually likes to experiment with a dead bait and then a live pinfish or pilchard, to see which is the lucky bait of the day.

By far the most popular method for targeting muttons is with a ballyhoo "plug" (minus head and tail), or a medium-sized live bait drifted over some sort of structure.

Pilchards, pinfish and mojarras all work fine as small live baits, but nothing works for muttons like a live or fresh-dead ballyhoo. Big snappers actually prefer crustaceans as their primary diet, so when using fish as bait, you're getting more of an opportunity bite here, rather than a natural prey reaction.

We always freeze some ballyhoo from previous trips to use as bait, while we wait for the "livies" to appear. Once the 'hoos appear in the slick, you can catch them with a No.16 long-shank hair hook baited with a small bit of peeled shrimp, or small strip of squid. Have your snapper rigs ready and put the first few live 'hoos out as you catch them. The smaller 'hoos are better. Add a few to the livewell as soon as possible; you never know when a pesky bird will appear and spook them away. (This includes cormorants, which are not shy about diving for their supper around boats.) I fish the baits in the grass with just enough weight to keep it on the bottom. Keep one reel locked up, and another rigged with a dropback setup. On the dropback rig, give a striking fish only a few feet to run, before closing the bail and crossing his eyes. SB

CHAPTER 10

Chum

"Capt. Ron Green"

ytripper

Why chum? There are few folks who can drive downwind of a cloud of barbecue smoke without turning their heads. If it's lunch time, there's a good chance they'll be turning into the parking lot.

It's the same with fish. They're spread out, but if they pass through a cloud of attractive fish or shellfish scent, or tiny morsels drifting downcurrent of a site, they'll likely ease in there for a better look. Creatures of habit, they're searching for a snack or even a hefty meal, just like people. Like barbecue smoke, they've had only enough to whet their appetites.

Anglers who refrain from chumming could be cutting back on their catch each day.

SNAPPER GROUPER   See DVD for more on chumming.

Anglers chum for yellow-tail snapper with bag in the water. They're drifting small, weightless baits far behind the boat.

Chumming Really Works

Chumming just naturally works to increase the action on a bottom fishing spot, especially on a slow day. When anchored over natural bottom or an artificial reef stretching for several acres, it only makes sense to entice the fish to within casting range.

Do it properly in a slow or moderate current, with a constant dribble of juicy items, and snapper and grouper will usually ease in closer below your boat. It's best to chum with small pieces; this attracts predators, instead of filling them up. As you deploy the chum, monitor direction and speed of the tidbits as they sink. The chum ideally will sink to the bottom near the boat, with more reef habitat just downtide. If the current is a little fast, you may have to fish far behind the boat, letting out line with a small, lead weight that will roughly match the chum's sink rate.

If the current is strong or the water too deep to allow surface chumming, place the chum in a weighted mesh bag and lower to the bottom for desired results. Some anglers keep inexpensive orange or grapefruit sacks on the boat for that very purpose. They can be weighted with a lead trolling ball, dive weights, an iron sash weight, even a brick. The sack should be over-weighted, instead of under; you want a sack that will easily hold bottom in the current. Attaching a mesh bag to the anchor rope is another trick. Used citrus bags can be discarded at day's end, back at the marina.

Fresh chum in the water will almost always attract fish to your baits from

BLOCK CHUM

Over the years, commercially made frozen chum blocks have become readily available at tackle shops and marinas. They're handy to use and generally inexpensive, but vary widely in quality. The best blocks have a greater proportion of menhaden, or some other oily, ground fish. They're easy to use, too: merely unwrap the block, drop in your mesh bag, and you're good to go.

Pure menhaden oil is great for mixing with small chunks of dog food, or small food pellets of some kind, that will sink down. Emulsified "menhaden milk" has also been developed that actually sinks in a white cloud. SB

Lucky angler works a nice fish up to the gaff. Anchoring off the coast and patiently chumming really does work.

downcurrent, and possibly from a short distance upcurrent.

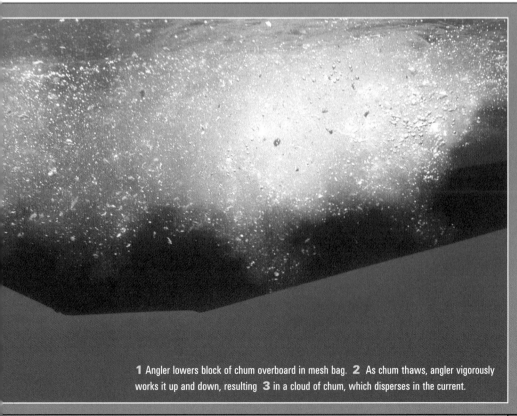

1 Angler lowers block of chum overboard in mesh bag. **2** As chum thaws, angler vigorously works it up and down, resulting **3** in a cloud of chum, which disperses in the current.

CHEAP CHUM

There's nothing like a mesh bag full of free shrimp heads, for attracting many species of fish. When action slows, mash the sack under a shoe (not a bare foot) several times and toss it back overboard while tied to a cleat. Shrimpheads should be cheap, since they're discarded by fish markets. In southern latitudes, most lobster heads are also discarded.

Using fish carcasses is legal and returns biomass to the reef.

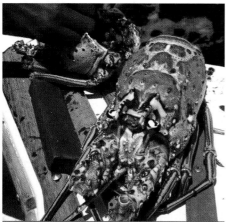

Bahamian islander utilizes leftover lobster heads, by pounding them up for chum for the coral reef just below his boat. Reef fish appreciate these offerings.

Crushing a bag of lobster heads will attract most fish living in a coral reef community. And, for those anglers with their own traps for blue crabs, the shells and other discarded crab parts, prior to boiling, also make a fine chum for many fish. Be sure to use plenty of ice here; shellfish parts spoil within hours.

It's even possible to chum with fish carcasses from the marina's cleaning table. One proven chum is sheepshead carcasses. Why? Grouper and snapper can't carry them off, but can only hang around, watching for something more bite-size. The chum smell will attract everything downcurrent, and possibly from a short distance upcurrent. More slender carcasses lying on bottom, such as trout, grunts and Spanish mackerel, will gradually disappear as grouper grab them and depart. A mesh bag of the same can be delivered to the bottom with a brick inside, but it's susceptible to damage from passing sharks. Especially nurse sharks, who nap under the very same ledges favored by grouper. Another trick is to use a heavy rod with several hooks and a pound of lead, that can lower two good-sized trout or mackerel carcasses to the bottom for a half hour (until they become water-logged). When finished with them, toss them in the motor well until ready to leave, then chop and drop overboard. Reef fish appreciate the gesture.

Chumming with whole fish carcasses is legal, and a good way to return biomass to the reef for other fish to consume (instead of leaving them floating around marinas, or feeding lazy pelicans). Carrying a bucket of fish carcasses offshore is also legal. But marine enforcement officers are quick to write a citation if fish fillets are found on the same boat. It isn't generally legal to clean fish offshore.

If you need fresh fish parts, bring your bucket around the cleaning table the evening before your departure. If you can't make it by sunset, call the marina ahead and ask them to leave a bucket under the cleaning table, with instructions for grunt, seabass, snapper, trout and Spanish mackerel carcasses. Be sure to ice the bucket overnight, to keep the chum fresh. A layer of ice over the top of the bucket, and then stored in a smaller boat chest overnight, is usually sufficient to keep it fresh. A friendly

Ladling out Special Chum for Yellowtail

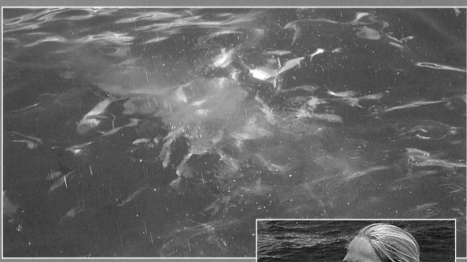

Serious YELLOWTAIL anglers mix their own chum the night before. A bucket or two of oats is soaked overnight in water, then mixed with several thawed chum blocks, with a few squirts of menhaden oil added. The "slop" is stirred with a stick, and stored in the boat in buckets with sealed lids (in case of choppy seas). Anchored on the reef, keep a mesh bag with a chum block in the water, but also ladle out the "slop" every few minutes. If the current isn't too slow or fast, the result can be a solid school of yellowtail snapper congregating astern. SB

marina manager may allow the chum bucket in his freezer room overnight, though it requires more time to thaw on the following day. Chum merely iced down is ready to use immediately. The frozen bucket is more practical for two- and three-day trips.

SHRIMPBOAT CULL AS CHUM

On the Gulf Coast especially, shrimpboat cull was for many years the easiest form of chum. You handed an empty bucket or two to a crewman on an anchored shrimpboat offshore, with some cold drinks or maybe a five dollar bill, and they loaded you up with small fish of many species, some squid and perhaps a few crabs. In the bayous or bays this was easier to pull off, since you weren't maneuvering the boat alongside much larger vessels in choppy seas. Even offshore, some smart boat handling could pull it off, even when the shrimpboat

was still pulling nets. There are risks in this maneuver, however. Bumping into a big shrimpboat usually means that the smaller boat earns a bruising. Falling overboard with a full bucket isn't advisable either, considering that hordes of hungry sharks often follow working shrimpboats. Buying chum blocks is decidedly less risky and time-consuming.

Down in the tropics, local fishermen don't waste their lobster heads and conch leftovers, when they have a fishing trip scheduled. They keep the leftovers cold if possible, anchor out over the reefs, and break up the lobster heads with anything handy, even a whetstone. Tropical snapper and grouper are quick to recognize lobster heads, and they'll come around to investigate. Anglers visiting in The Bahamas or Caribbean should save their lobster heads, or those from nearby divers at least, and try them when anchored on the reefs.

Above, shrimpboat bycatch utilized for chum. Below, traveler chums with canned jack mackerel while visiting The Bahamas. Right, spring-loaded chum chopper slices and dices available fish scraps and bait.

CHOPPING CHUM

You can either spend hours manually cutting chum on a board and tossing it overboard, or go high-tech. Storing a chum machine on a boat adds some hassle, but once anchored and set up, these little babies can crank out the good stuff. One device is called the Chum Churn. The PVC pipe is filled with whatever smaller fish products are available, and hung over the side of the boat. A spring-loaded, hand-operated plunger device armed with sharp blades inside the pipe churns and cuts the fish to pieces, dropping them overboard. The blades easily cut through fish bones and crabs.

Here's the prize: a fine mutton snapper.

Another device is called Mister Chummer, made by Fish-NG Accessories. It's a number 32 size, hand-operated meat grinder. This one has a rodholder-mount and cutting board as separate accessories. Elec-Tra-Mate also makes a motorized chum grinder of the same size with a gimbal rod mount; it works on a boat's 12-volt DC system. Some anglers also make their own chum at home, using meatgrinders obtained from restaurant suppliers or hunting outfitters.

LIVE CHUM

In some of the more remote, lightly fished areas, sizeable grouper and snapper inhabit rockpiles and reefs as shallow as 10 feet. It's here that live chumming, often with pilchards or some other small, flashy species, can ignite spectacular and rarely seen surface bites. When these fish are aggressively chasing live chum, a plug or fly caster can enjoy the opportunity to hook up on topwater action. Veteran live chummers advise against throwing more than a half dozen or so baits at a time. It's best to entice but not satiate your quarry here. SB

FOR MANGROVES AND MUTTONS

Chumming can be vital for cautious mangroves and mutton snapper. That's why some experts use 8 to 12 boxes of frozen chum per trip. As they arrive on the spot, they drop a chum block in a bag with ½-inch holes, tie it to a boat cleat and circle the spot, watching their bottom machine for fish signs.

"For mutton snapper, you should have your chum in the sack ready to deploy before making a half-circle around the reef," says George Mitchell. "Keep the boat a good 50 feet from the target spot, a sand ring that typically surrounds a high-profile coral head. Start chumming as the boat passes by, and squirt a bit of menhaden oil overboard. Circle the reef, then head upcurrent to drop anchor. Anchor a good 200 feet upcurrent. There are two reasons for that: First, you can swivel your engines or change cleats on the anchor line, to fine-tune your position. Secondly, you can start your chumslick close to the sand ring. As ballyhoo appear, take in some anchor line, easing the boat farther from the hard reef, to lessen the chance of a big fish breaking your line.

"Typically, channel muttons are passing through and it takes chum to keep them around. Frozen chum works, and live pilchards. Smaller pilchards work best because the average mutton here is under 12 pounds. Toss a handful of pilchards and wait to see if there are surface boils that look like snappers.

"Drop a chum sack in the channel with frozen menhaden. If the water is in the low 70s or high 60s, use a sack with ¼-inch holes. If the water is warm, use a fine-mesh sack. Add a couple of squirts of menhaden oil to the slick every few minutes, and that should get the ballyhoo back there in the slick." SB

CHAPTER 11

Electronics

Finding well-hidden snapper and grouper is rarely an easy task on a featureless body of water. That's why almost all offshore captains today, at the very least, use a bottom machine and GPS unit. Add a VHF radio for safety, and that's the minimum dashboard package advised for anyone who hopes to catch high-quality bottom fish.

Add-on options are many. One favorite is the GPS chartplotter function, which makes it unnecessary to heave an old-fashioned buoy in the water, when that honeyhole is finally found.

Certainly worth the cost. As we point out in this chapter, fish-finding electronics are a small but important investment in the overall cost of owning and operating a boat.

When bottom fishing, so very much depends on using good marine electronics to get you to the honeyholes.

See DVD for more electronics tips.

Using Marine Electronics

Coral reefs in clear water and tall oil and gas platforms on the Gulf's horizon make it easy for people to catch bottom fish without electronics. Finding these fish in murky or deeper, open water is another matter, of course. After finding a good spot by one

Learning to read the difference in bottom structure is the real ticket to catching fish.

means or another, fishermen naturally want to return. That means navigating back to a small patch of water on a featureless expanse of water, then narrowing the search to determine *exactly* where to drop anchor.

This little trick requires a global positioning system (GPS) navigation unit and then a bottom machine, as a minimum. Both can be installed while the boat is on a trailer or tied to the dock, and the cost can be as low as about $400, if you skimp on a few options. If doubts exist about proper installation, it's best to find the local marine electronics guru who can help out.

Snapper and grouper fishermen in Texas and

Louisiana easily went without these items for two generations, and some still do, because they have production platforms dotting the horizon. There were (and still are) lots of tall landmarks up to 90 miles offshore, at least on days with decent visibility, and most platforms are fairly easy to fish around. But today many boats there have switched to electronics, in the interest of straight-line navigation, regardless of visibility, and in finding offshore rocks and secret wrecks others don't know about. The rest of the country relies on navigating offshore without these handy landmarks. That's why navigating with compass and charts, after hundreds of years, is beginning to be a lost art. Why? Easy-to-use electronics are now widely sold.

On the other end of the scale, it's been observed that some of the new generation of fishermen jump into boats and high-tech navigation gear, but many never actually learn the basics of a compass or charts. Instead, they watch for the arrow on their GPS to show them the way. If the machine goes out, or the satellite signal is jammed because the military

Capt. George Mitchell watches the electronics mounted inside his console, out of the weather.

is playing games offshore, these fishermen may look like kids lost in the big city. They don't have even a general sense of east and west, because it turns out they've been ignoring the built-in compass that came with their boat. If electronic navigation systems ever malfunction while offshore, one should always have a paper chart (in a plastic tube) or a waterproof chart of the immediate area, and a good-sized compass professionally mounted on the dash.

That's all you need to return, if you can draw a line from roughly where you are back to port, and parallel it with the "compass rose" on the paper chart. Roses are the 360-degree circles showing all points of the compass, and they're handily scattered on quality charts.

Meanwhile, it's best to make sure the boat captain you fish with knows a few tricks about electronics, before going snapper or grouper fishing. Here's what some of our Florida captains have to say:

RICK RYALS

For locating fishing spots, I still use Loran C because I've got 30 years worth of numbers (fishing spots) from roaming around out there. However, I can't urge anglers strongly enough to learn navigation with a good GPS. It's faster and more accurate than Loran. It will also be around much longer, since Loran is going to be phased out.

Make sure you learn how to use your GPS's

A well-equipped boat prowls off the coast, its captain watching his bottom machine for tell-tale structure below.

Captain Rick Ryals with his dash-mounted setup. Gag grouper, below, hang around small bottom breaks.

chartplotter function. For precise anchoring, it's better than my silly marker buoy and once learned, it's more effective. But carry the buoy with you, just in case.

Your bottom machine is very important, and everybody has a favorite brand. I use a full color machine, and it shows me the difference in bait versus big fish. Color, however, isn't necessary. A good chrome or black-and-white machine will show everything you need and then some. Remember, learning to read the difference in *bottom structure* is the real ticket, not how many fish it will show you. It's also important to take the time when you get your scope installed, to make sure you'll be able to read it at high speed. Learning to find underwater spots when a boat is running at planing speed is critical to your hunting skills. You can search a lot more ground at fairly high speed, instead of idling the boat around.

Fortunately for the beginning offshore angler, there are many resources for finding starter fishing spots. They're called "numbers"—either longitude and latitude coordinates, or older Loran-C numbers. The former are found with a GPS, the cost of which continues to drop. There are lists of published GPS numbers that include some great spots that even the pros visit. *Florida Sportsman* magazine, for instance, has a great series of charts, each compiled by local experts.

As the great Capt. Fred Morrow of Mayport would say, "It's hard to catch fish, once they're already in some other captain's box." In other words, the best way to find a honeyhole is to search for it yourself. The published fishing spots offshore have already seen many hooks. They can offer great fishing after a storm passes, for instance, but on any given Saturday, they can be pretty tough places to find quality bottom fish.

Many of the older commercial snapper fishermen talk about the early 1970s with some reverence. That's when the U.S. Coast Guard turned off the Loran-A transmitting stations, forcing snapper fishermen out of their ruts, and on a search to find new snapper bottom. Morrow said they began making up to 50 stops each day; they stopped at every little bottom irregularity that appeared on their bottom machines, and were rewarded with many previously untouched areas, spots that very likely had *never known a fish hook.* Amazing catches were made. But it only happened because boat captains were forced into a search mode.

Look at it this way. Every offshore number somebody gives you, or you see on a chart, has already been fished by others. If you spend time looking for your own spots and find a few, the rewards will be considerable.

The downside is that there are almost no shortcuts when it comes to finding new bottom. It's strictly a matter of putting in your time scanning with a bottom machine. However, as a tip, I do seem to find most of my spots within a mile or so of spots I already have. That's because each limestone formation offshore is often part of a bigger geological pattern. Find a good shelf or ledge, and chances are there's more within the same zip code.

The better captains operating within 30 miles of either coast will always take different routes to their next stop, looking for new spots. The problem for them is that most nearshore areas are heavily charted, and as a result are heavily fished. I've personally had the best luck searching for new spots in 120 to 150 feet of water. One could argue that is the depths where I spend most of my time searching with confidence, but you'll have to solve that riddle yourself.

Bottom machines are the only way to interpret various structures far below, where fish gather.

tight rope. Make your first stop by anchoring just upwind of your fishing spot. Before pulling anchor to move to the next spot, check the true direction of your anchor line. If the compass reads 165 degrees while you sit at anchor, then you'd better plan for the next couple of hours on anchoring 165 degrees away from your next spot. That's far more accurate than going by a boat's wind drift. Remember to check your anchor heading each time before you pick up anchor. Why is that? Wind and tide vary throughout the

GARY FOLDEN

A good compass will not only assist you in getting to and from your desired fishing spot, but can also be used in anchoring each time you stop. Wind and current are the two key factors that determine the heading (where your bow points), when the boat finally lays at anchor on a

Find a good shelf or ledge, and chances are there are more in the same zip code.

Those who can read their bottom machines may find schools of fish.

Gary Folden prefers the older paper-fed bottom recorders. His electronics are mounted overhead, out of the weather.

Snapper and scamp grouper prowl one of the Gulf's sunken tugboats in 100 feet.

day. An offshore breeze can shift 360 degrees in a day's outing, and 90 to 180 degrees is common and rather expected as the tides change and the afternoon breeze kicks in.

Having a GPS unit on board will permit the captain to do three important things—especially in bad visibility such as fog: It will get you out there, will locate some known fishing spots, and return you to port. Learn three or four basic functions of these units, and you're on your way to better fishing. Spending an hour at home going over the instruction booklet can make a huge difference.

The fishfinder is your view of the world below and remains such a crucial element in bottom fishing. A good fishfinder will show you the contour of the bottom and differentiate between soft (sand or mud) and hard (rock) bottom. It even shows the soft growth such as sponges, and also baitfish schools. The sophisticated machines available today not only show fish, but their size and relative numbers. The new LCD fishfinders have a high pixel count and offer great resolution on the screen. If your budget permits, go for the high wattage, color machines and remember that transducer installation is critical. Transducers are the isolated element that beams a signal underwater. They're mounted either in the bilge below deck, or on the boat's transom. Make sure it points straight down and not off to the side.

Happy angler lands a pair of snapper on a bottom rig.

"You might run over (and mark) a cone of fish out there, where they were *really* congregated." Ralph Delph

RALPH DELPH

Often we can spot a single fish with the depth recorder, and all it takes is some practice. I personally think 600 watts per unit is good enough. Mine is 1,000 watts, however, with plenty of extra power. I also favor the split screen with two images. The wide angle is for finding fish. We use from 50 to 200 kilohertz for positioning the boat over the top. That puts you close. But you want to be accurate. There seems to be a critical zone of five feet, whether or not you get a strike. In clear water we've seen fish come up 100 feet to grab a bait, or go down 100 to grab it. They'll easily grab it 60 to 70 feet above bottom. You can actually see it on the bottom machine, the fish rising up to meet a bucktail jig.

It certainly pays to watch that machine while running. With today's equipment it's the first thing I turn on in the morning, and one of the last I turn off. Even in the old days when we used paper recorders, we turned them on for miles at a time. You might run over a cone of fish out there, where they were really congregated. They might be muttons or groupers, or maybe all gags. We would print up a big wad of fish on that paper. No bottom features were

A weekend crowd converged on this spot.
Bottom machines helped them decide where to anchor.

Finding Spots Offshore

Anglers searching offshore for good bottom are advised to buy at least one chart of the coast or island they plan to fish. Study the charts carefully for clues on where to fish. Most, but not all, will have a few public GPS numbers.

The big NOAA charts utilize a series of abbreviations to represent various types of fishing spots: "co" is used for coral, "sh" for shell and "obstr" for obstruction, which is often an artificial reef. Wrecks are indicated with a symbol that looks like the outline of a boat, with ribs included. Also, keep an eye out for the abbreviation "PA" which is often used for "position approximate." These spots may carry clues about areas that have been forgotten or ignored by the public. They may be worth a visit or two, a check with today's modern bottom machines.

Experienced offshore captains stay alert for unusual fish signs while running the boat across miles of open water. For instance, a surfacing turtle may mark a ledge or wreck, since turtles nap beneath protective bottom structure.

These same captains also watch for fish signs, even an upwelling of water where a strong current collides with a wreck. Blue runners often school on the surface over these rocks and wrecks, as do smaller baitfish. The presence of spadefish finning on the surface in calm weather often means a metal wreck is just below.

If you have LORAN numbers, the only true way to convert them accurately to GPS is to stop and fish there, with both electronic units running on the boat. By hitting the "event" button on the GPS, one can ensure an exact return in the future. LORAN is scheduled to be phased out, though they keep pushing back the phase-out date. Many of the computer conversion tables that are used for converting LORAN numbers to GPS may get you close to the spot, but will still require a search.

Searching for a spot likely means dropping a buoy on the old LORAN number, and running a search pattern. The buoy is thrown and then circled, ideally with the distance to the buoy widening slowly but consistently in a spiral pattern. There are no guarantees when running a search, but it does help to have a good bottom machine set on split-screen image, scanning as much of the bottom as possible.

Other means exist for getting offshore numbers. They can be traded like baseball cards, for instance, while the astute angler keeps several of the best ones for himself. In addition to getting a beginner's set of numbers from a chart like *Florida Sportsman*, you can often get numbers from coastal fishing clubs or even buy a published set of numbers.

Another method of finding new areas to fish is by watching where others bottom fish. Don't approach too close, however. If you can read their lips, that's probably too close, and you probably don't want to hear what they're saying anyway. Mark your location and try to guess the distance to the other boat's location.

In many cases, just finding the *area* is good enough. If you come back another day and look around, you may find structure holding fish.

Older captains who are getting out of the business can also be approached and directly asked for numbers. Any number of tactics can be used to accomplish this goal: a steak dinner, a trade-out of future fish for the table, or an outright fee for the numbers. Everything is negotiable. SB

discernible, it was just flat bottom, but there was something about the spot that draws those fish. The commercial guys have been doing this sort of thing for years. Sharks would be there too; they were just big gatherings of fish, a real bonanza to find. If you treat a spot like that real nice and don't take too many fish, it will last the rest of your life. Over the years I've found many hundreds of waypoints offshore, quite a list. Today we can go back to these spots and hit a good fish, then move on to the next one. In this way they quickly replenish themselves, and you've got more fish out there than you ever dreamed of."

DENNIS YOUNG

Folks serious about going offshore for bottom fish should buy a color bottom machine. They can tell different species of fish on bottom, and that saves time. Color also tells big baitfish from little baits. A cloud of glass minnows down there doesn't have much appeal, compared with cigar minnows. With black and white bottom units, you can see bottom and clouds of bait, but can't even tell what they are. Color is so much better. Also buy a quality VHF radio and antenna. Guys that buy a $30 antenna will find they're not that reliable or have that good a distance. A splash-proof radio is such a great thing; they're going to get wet on center console boats, but a good, waterproof radio just becomes part of the dash.

As for finding new bottom, look for a transducer setup that offers a crystal clear picture at 30 knots, no electronic interference from bubbles. The ideal high-speed transducer is a dome through-hull system. My brother has one and he fell in love with it. The dome looks like a teardrop and is filled with liquid, something like linseed oil. He typically finds two or three new spots on every trip. Not just bottom with a couple of fish or some bait, but real spots worth anchoring on. He's a commercial fisherman out of Destin. He fishes between Panama City and Orange Beach, Alabama.

Half my secret spots, and all the best ones, have come from running over new areas with my eyes fixed on the bottom machine. I've found spots from four to 50 miles offshore, and all the miles in between. SB

All depthfinders (bottom units) have automatic settings, and for many fishermen, it's easier just to leave the unit set on auto during every trip. However, conditions underwater change, and that often requires adjustments that an auto setting may

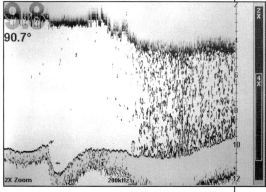

not notice or adjust to. Auto settings tune out some information in order to present a clean screen picture, which may ignore water temperature thermoclines and small schools of bait, among other things.

Capt. George LaBonte says to begin each day, one should always start by setting their Gain to basic operation. After getting powered up and reaching the water depth you intend to fish, note the depth, and then double the range setting. A 50-foot depth should

be set at about 120 feet on the bottom machine.

Then, crank up the Gain until a second or false bottom appears. With the range set for 120 feet, and actual depth at 50, the second bottom line will appear at about 100 feet.

Continue cranking up the Gain until static appears between the surface, and 50-foot line. That's when its time to back off a little on the Gain, until only a hint of interference is still visible. A little interference is acceptable from five to 10 feet down, and bottom fishermen at this depth don't really need to detect fish there.

Then, switch the Range setting back to 50 or 60 feet. Now you're at the maximum output, with the least amount of interference. Finding that optimal Gain setting is the most basic step to getting that recorder to work for you.

TRANSDUCERS

Transducers are easily the single-most important item in your fish-hunting gear. Without properly tracing the bottom and fish above it, there is no way to interpret what is down there. The transducer emits sonic waves that bounce off bottom structure, and return to your boat for interpretation. How the transducer is attached to your boat, and the strength and frequency of the signals it broadcasts, makes a very big difference in fish-finding ability.

Most common choices are 50 to 200 kilohertz, because they represent the average needs of most fishermen. Choosing higher or lower frequencies would mean someone has very specific requirements they're looking for, that go beyond the needs of almost all fishermen. The 50 kHz setting is fine for deep-dropping in 1,000 feet of water, for instance, and it easily zooms in for a closeup of the bottom itself. (Often there's no need to view anything out there, except the last few feet above bottom). The 200 kHz works in shal-

Top, a high gain setting will mark more fish, but it's harder to read. Below, red grouper hides near structure.

low water, all the way down to 300 feet. The two depth ranges pretty much cover about 98 percent of all bottom fishermen. So, 50 to 200 kHz is perfect for most boat owners.

How boaters jazz up their wattage power on their bottom machine units is up to them, of course. Some units go up to 1,000 watts, others even more.

Most units are powered at 600 watts, which handles the needs of most boaters. Some of the captains who constantly fish in 200 feet and more, who really refine their efforts on a day-to-day basis, insist on using 1,000-watt machines.

It's okay to send out a strong signal with high wattage, but using the right frequency is really essential. Most people use (or should use) a split-screen image, using the lower, 50 kHz frequency to search, since it broadcasts a wide cone to the bottom. The more narrow, 200 kHz broadcasts a narrow band, and it's good for "getting the goods" on a smaller area, defining the target, like a small wreck, and the fish around it. Split screen images are a little distracting, since it's easier to focus your attention on one constant picture of the bottom, while also driving the boat and watching for floating obstacles. It's little wonder many captains look tired by the end of the day. Even cheap bottom units have dual frequency. For those who shrink away from the two-picture screen, and favor single frequency (one picture only), the 200 kHz handles almost all of their needs, except in deep water.

Transducer quality varies widely. For instance, some of the commercial boats have transducers that cost thousands of dollars. Serious bottom fishermen should invest in one they can live with, that does a good job.

Which Mount is Right for You?

Three types of transducer exist. All are connected by cable to the bottom machine mounted on the boat's dashboard.

One transducer shoots THROUGH THE BOAT HULL, by mounting it down in the bilge. You basically dry the bilge out and glue the thing down, pointing it ideally straight down, and with no air pocket in the seal. Mount it close to the centerline keel of the boat, without making it shoot through the thicker keel itself. (Keep in mind that you can't shoot sonar signals through foam cored hulls.) Mount it toward the stern, since you don't want that part of the hull popping loose from the water, creating interference on your screen up above. There's nothing like a snow pattern on the TV screen, just as you pass over a new wreck loaded with fish.

The second transducer mounts on your boat's OUTER TRANSOM, out there in the water with a lot of turbulence around. It shoots a very clean signal, if the boat isn't going too fast, and especially if it isn't backing down through a wall of bubbles (back to your marker buoy, after dropping anchor.) It's a little known secret, but bubbles are the enemy of all transducers and bottom machines. They cloud the entire picture.

The third transducer requires cutting a hole in the bottom of your boat, and installing a THROUGH-HULL MOUNT. Many people are squeamish about drilling holes below the waterline in a perfectly good boat, and they manage to resist this idea. These mounts are, however, said to broadcast the cleanest signal. They are not inhibited by shooting sonic waves through solid boat fiberglass or other material, and also avoid the turbulence found farther astern around the transom. Many boatyards install them for around $500. SB

CHAPTER 12

Partyboat
Players

Bottom fishermen in the Gulf and South Atlantic states have a long tradition with "partyboats" going back many years. Today's boats are a safe, inexpensive way to fish far offshore, with no worries about making it back home. A solid, steel boat of a hundred feet or so is good insurance against sudden weather changes. During winter when the weather can change for the worse, big partyboats are almost infinitely safer than small boats. Why? A dunk in frigid water can turn into hypothermia and a real disaster in less than an hour, because rescue normally takes a lot longer than that. Even veteran offshore fishermen with fine boats often refrain from using them in winter, while the partyboats just keep on going.

Many of today's partyboats are state-of-the-art and a world removed from the older boats, up to and including vessels used only a few years ago.

Tasty mangrove snapper caught way offshore in winter, marked with stringers and angler ID numbers on a partyboat.

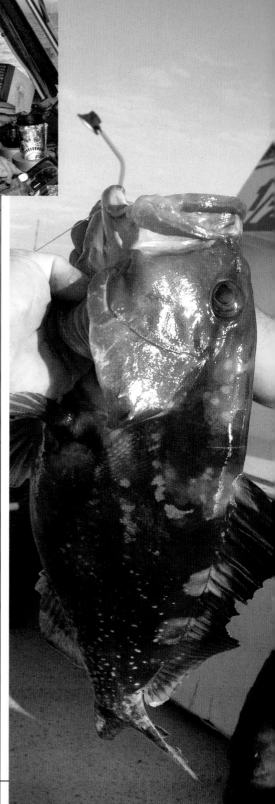

A veteran partyboat captain out of St. Petersburg, Florida watches an array of sonar and navigation gear. He is positioning his big vessel for an anchor drop for an early morning bite.

Above, anglers probe the depths. At right, deckhand accepts a red grouper for stringer and the cooler.

Partyboat Veterans Keep on Going

In the early morning light, a deckhand runs by with a big gaff, and fishermen scramble out of his way. Someone on the stern has another 20-pound grouper hooked up, and the poor fellow is hanging on for dear life, his rod pulled mostly over the rail. He'll have his hands full for the next 10 minutes; that fish is 150 feet below. The rest of us grab more fresh, live pinfish from our private little baitwells, re-bait and lower them down. The grouper bite has started, and it's game time. Up on the bow, we're a hundred feet away from the hooked fish, so there is little concern about crossing lines with the lucky angler.

Partyboats, often called "headboats," charge by the head and serve a fine purpose in hauling anglers young and old offshore for a shot at quality bottom fish—while charging a minimal price compared to actually owning a boat.

They're a great way for beginners, including teenagers, to find out if they have a taste for offshore bottom fishing. For others, it's the only affordable option if they don't own a boat, or have friends with boats. At the older end of partyboat patrons are the occasional salty veter-

This angler appears to be "rocked up" by a big fish and is strumming his line to annoy the fish.

ans now retired, who sign up aboard partyboats almost every week, sometimes fishing until they literally drop in their tracks. Some of these guys have signed "do not resuscitate" orders if they should collapse on deck, preferring to pass away fishing rather than in some nursing home.

Partyboats themselves may be a dying breed, however. The cost of running a quality operation gets tougher every year. In 2000 there were only 88 partyboats left in Florida, the number diminishing each year, with a moratorium on new permits in the Gulf. Insurance, fishery regulations, Coast Guard requirements, and general cost overhead (including fuel and crew) are more expensive or restrictive than in previous years. Many boats are state of the art and a world removed from the older boats, up to and including the 1980s.

Only a few years ago, anglers who signed aboard a partyboat were basically left to fend for themselves. There might not be air conditioning, and chain smokers could keep the cabin foggy. They might keep the lights on all night, playing cards and drinking whiskey. Sleeping the night away in bus seats in six-foot seas was a tricky affair and none too restful. Especially sitting with strangers. If you were lucky, there was an unshaven cook with a lit cigarette, flipping greasy eggs for breakfast and burgers for lunch. Outside on deck, rental tackle was usually adequate, but one-dimensional. You lowered several baited hooks to the bottom with a big lead weight on 80-pound line, and waited for a bite. Bait was a washtub full of thawed, purple squid, cheap menhaden, leftover bonito, shrimpboat cull, whatever was available. Snapper and grouper were dropped into a personal grass sack tied to your spot at the rail. The fish in each sack turned pale and white in the

This angler is 92 years old and still keeps fishing partyboats. This gag grouper gave him a real tussle.

Partyboat angler leans hard on a big fish, using the rail for leverage. His custom reel sports a huge handle.

hot summer sun, before being tossed into an overworked freezer for the ride back. Even the sacks turned a little ripe after constant use.

The captain fished without GPS, using dead reckoning (running time multiplied by engine RPMs, which was a crude speedometer). He might have Loran A, which was inaccurate, or later, Loran C. A buoy with a flag marked the spot, and could be circled for a good distance while searching for others. Weather predictions were often inaccurate. There were no offshore buoy reports or regional radar via the Internet. In fact, there are lots of high-tech innovations taken for granted today that didn't exist then.

Today's partyboats have precise navigation gear and they can find and park over an offshore object the size of a small house. At least, an experienced captain and deckhand can do so.

So, why are fewer partyboats making trips offshore? People today demand more comfort and service, according to an industry spokesman. They like the faster, classier boats. And they're quick to complain if they don't get it, or they won't return. The better companies are constantly fine-tuning their operation to accommodate people, and they listen to suggestions.

Some anglers don't mind the lack of elbow room on a partyboat; they meet new people on each new trip.

Several people are hooked up here, on a calm and perfect day. The shade is nice during summer, too.

Tips on Picking Partyboats

There are a few tips one may ponder, before signing on for a trip off-shore on these vessels:

If you've never been offshore before, a good place to start is on a half-day or full-day trip. In most cases these are smaller boats and are the least expensive. The down side is you rarely catch keeper-size snap-per or grouper. If you feel you're ready to spend a few days on a headboat, then you're ready to catch some real fish. Long-range boats come in a variety of sizes and travel with as few as six anglers, and as many as 50. As you can imagine, they're not all created equal. A boat that's been fishing out of the same marina for a number of years is probably a safe bet. To check out partyboats, message boards on the Internet are one avenue that's become available, such as as the one on www.floridasportsman.com.

People look for added value, more fishing time with less running (voyage) time. They like a clean boat run in a professional manner.

The better partyboats today hire crew members who are people-friendly, not just people with fishing experience. Deckhands who can untangle lines in a quick and friendly fashion, who promptly ice down the catch, who deflate undersized fish before releasing them, who can give a safety lecture, or friendly tips on how to hook and catch more fish.

Meanwhile, boats run in a sloppy fashion continue to drop out. Those that aren't safety-conscious often wind up with an injured angler, and the boat could lose its insurance, if it had any coverage at all. One has to be rather careful when handling large numbers of the public, especially when going to sea, in today's litigious society.

Some partyboats in a high-tourist destination merely spend a day on the water, anchoring and dropping baits, and if fish are caught, that's a good thing. They may lack the time to run offshore to a remote area with more available fish, or they may not want to lose tackle over rough bottom and wrecks. This phenomenon is common with the half-day trips, whose boats seldom lose sight of land. The spots they fish usually see lots of fishing pressure. Still, one never knows what they'll catch. A 20-pound grouper or snapper is always a possibility. Sharks and other sights can be thrillers to the uninitiated. And who can guess the value of taking kids fishing offshore for the first time on a seaworthy partyboat?

For the slightly older crowd who are considering buying an offshore boat, the big partyboats give people a chance to try their hand at fishing beyond sight of land. They can see if they like it, have a feel or a hunger for more, before making an expen-

sive investment in new fiberglass.

And there are always those who worry about losing sight of land in small craft. Running around offshore in a small boat has no appeal to them at all, while a hundred tons of partyboat beneath those shoes feels like good insurance.

For your best chance at catching legal-sized snapper and grouper, the longer trips, the overnighters lasting two or three days offshore,

What to Bring?

A few items found on a partyboat veteran's checklist might include snacks, a rough hand towel or two, needlenose pliers and a bait knife. One will also need an ice chest to leave in the car, to haul the fish home. Don't forget cash for the cook's galley or tipping the deckhands at journey's end. You might bring a small bait-cutting board of 18 inches or so, and a flat, small tacklebox that will hold a variety of hooks and lead weights. Deck clutter is kept to a minimum, so leave the big tacklebox full of Lucky-13s and Crazy Crawlers back at the house. A 5-gallon bucket may be very handy for hauling your gear on board. And, a favorite pillow and light blanket may aid a great deal in napping or sleeping on the longer trips. A light sleeping bag is wonderful in winter. Don't forget a hat, and at least a light jacket. The air conditioning may be too cold, or the weather could turn chilly or rainy offshore.

A longer, stiff rod for casting may have an

A warsaw grouper caught in early spring aboard a Texas partyboat.

offshore, the overnight trips offer great value.

offer great value. These trips may result in a thousand or more total pounds of fish, especially if the boat is grandfathered in to bringing home two-day bag limits. Boats running to the Dry Tortugas and Middle Grounds are prime examples.

A good captain will try to put everyone on grouper and snapper, and will then stop at a favorite wreck to top off on big amberjack limits. Incidental bottom fish such as porgies, mar-

gate, triggerfish and grunts are bonus bottom fish. And, one can always "free-line" off the stern with a weightless bait, for pelagic types such as kingfish, dolphin and cobia. That trick normally requires a longer rod for casting, with a reel that doesn't backlash easily. Keep in mind that some boats don't allow overhead casting at all, since a number of anglers have been smacked on the head or even knocked out by flailing tackle. SB

Savvy anglers wear a "scope patch" on their neck or take a motion sickness pill before even leaving the dock.

advantage over stubbier bottom tackle. If a bonus cobia or dolphin swims by at 20 yards, an 8-foot fiberglass rod, with a spinning or casting reel full of 40-pound line, and armed with a 3-ounce jig, will easily reach out. Whether that fish can be landed without wrapping a dozen other lines remains to be seen. It may require some fancy footwork and cooperation from oth-

ers. However, boatless anglers have landed 50-pound kingfish with this gear, and won offshore tournaments while aboard partyboats. And found themselves with a new offshore boat for first prize.

Check out each partyboat's Website or brochure. Both should provide valuable tips on how that particular boat operates. SB

CHAPTER 13

Making the Long Run

Many anglers are good for at least one big adventure each summer, running the boat to some hard-to-reach spot you normally wouldn't try on a casual weekend. A destination that requires planning and foresight. This means overnight considerations, a boat checklist, serious fishing in some faraway spot (or country) where the fish are bigger and there isn't competition on the horizon. It also means lots of fishing time in three days and nights, the equivalent of an entire summer on the water for some people.

Running to The Bahamas isn't difficult for small boats when the weather is good. You will always have a lee shoreline to fish or rest. A Middle Grounds trip, however, requires constant seamanship.

Grouper action of this
caliber doesn't happen
often in heavily fished
waters. Often, it means
making a long run.

Fishing Far Distant Waters

Taking young anglers on long trips offshore carries some risks. Some become burned out from the long hours and discomfort, while others are hooked for life on this sport.

Anglers who are gung-ho for snapper and grouper have pretty much perfected making those long runs to The Bahamas, Middle Grounds, Dry Tortugas and the 100-fathom curve. In Northeast Florida, they run to the dropoff ledges "only" 50 miles out in the Atlantic, where the Gulf Stream passes by. In the Western Gulf, folks from Louisiana and Texas have for years been running up to 90 miles out to the deepwater platforms and rocky peaks that are sometimes covered up with grouper and oversized red snapper—places seldom visited by recreational anglers.

That seems to be the appeal, fishing in far-flung places where the water is always blue, and the crowds never go. These runs carry inherent risks from the weather, because the sea commands respect. Caught far from land, even the best boats can take a good beating when the weather turns ugly. It's a sport not meant for everyone, but there are anglers with a hungry heart who will always push the envelope. On a bad enough day offshore, this may even qualify for "extreme sport" status.

Most of these runs that take you to the less-fished spots are so far offshore, they call for an overnight stay—to make it worth the trouble and fuel of getting out there. In most cases it makes no sense to beat your way offshore for four hours, and fish two or three before returning the same day. Fishing time is at least quadrupled when one spends the night out there, and it doesn't cost a penny more for fuel. More bait perhaps, but few anglers mind paying for that when the fish are biting fast and furious.

DIFFERENT BALL GAME

The overnight stay does carry some risks. In safe harbor in the Tortugas or Bahamas, that's a piece of cake. Moored all night to a solid steel platform in the Central or Western Gulf, there is aid or at least solid footing only a few

A boat of at least 26 feet, well-equipped with a strong hull, is highly recommended when making the long runs offshore.

feet away, though a watch must be kept on currents and winds that can reverse, trapping the boat beneath solid steel. However, at the Middle Grounds or the deep ledges out beyond, or out in the Atlantic, most boats are simply on their own. One is at the mercy of the weather, and passing boat and ship traffic. Out there, a pair of seaworthy vessels traveling together is about the best insurance one can hope for.

Anglers 20 years ago got away with fishing the Gulf or Atlantic in far smaller boats than are commonly seen out there today. Some people weren't so lucky, and U.S. coastal waters are littered with the sunken wrecks of small boats that didn't return to port. Some were caught in bad weather, but many sank for simple reasons that could have been avoided. A bilge pump quit after a thru-hull fitting sprang loose, or someone backed into the swell with a low-transom boat. Perhaps a swamping happened during a sudden summer thunderstorm. It doesn't take much.

Salty veterans still around today sometimes shake their heads and wonder how they survived so long offshore years ago without a VHF radio and other safety equipment. Today's modern boating, navigational and engine technology improvements make these long runs safer and safer. Convenient information from offshore weather buoys on the Internet might be taken for granted today, but it seems hard to believe they weren't available until after the March 1993 storm. Today's Internet radar imagery shows cloud movements and they update every 20 minutes. There is even satellite imagery that shows water temperatures offshore. Of course a sudden summer thunderstorm, with downshear and high winds, is still difficult to predict.

CAMPING OUT ON THE FISH

The rewards of running far offshore in fine weather are worth it. Fishing a great spot without another boat on the horizon, and hungry, oversized fish below is a joy many anglers hope for, but don't always find. Perhaps they should; there are many more seaworthy, high-tech boats available today that are fast enough to visit the spots 50 to 100 miles offshore. As some, offshore veterans would say, "That's where the big ones bite."

There are advantages to making long boat runs to the Dry Tortugas, says Andy Griffiths, who owns several charterboats out of Stock Island near Key West. His 43-foot boats nor-

mally stay out for three days, so he's very familiar with overnight offshore trips. He says they're fishing at the best times of day, which is normally sunrise and sunset. You're also fishing at night, which is best of all for such species as mangrove snapper. He says on a single day trip, how are you going to catch anything when bottomfish are biting only at night during certain phases of the moon?

"If the fish are only biting at night, we're right there on top of them," says Griffiths. "On a three-day trip, you've got an entire day away from civilization, which is very relaxing. So you can slow down and lose some stress, which is something many people have forgotten about when fishing offshore. We fish all around the Tortugas or Marquesas, often anchoring in sheltered water at night, if we already have a lot of fish. Our boats sleep six anglers. There's nothing like getting a little experience on these long runs, or talking with the guys who already go, before making the same trip with your own boat."

Griffiths says they don't always anchor to sleep inside the National Park in the Tortugas. It's got to be chunky weather outside for that, and if

> **A trip to the Middle Grounds can be better than you've ever dreamt.**

Aerial view of Fort Jefferson. Though 70 miles from Key West, this place offers shelter for boaters.

chum. If it's winter, keep in mind you don't have to fish as far west of Key West. It has to be pretty darn good winter weather for us to fish all the way to the Tortugas. The Marquesas are good then, and we can anchor inside that island at night when we need to. You sleep better when anchored in calm water."

As for visiting Florida's **Middle Grounds**, that's one of the toughest long runs for overnight trips, with no safe harbors. It's completely exposed to the weather. There is no shelter, as with the Dry Tortugas or Bahamas. Anglers running far offshore of Louisiana or Texas run the gamut of cruel weather, but at least they have countless production platforms to moor to, or seek help from. At the Middle Grounds or the dropoffs farther offshore to the south and west, there is nothing but empty water.

Capt. Kevin McMillan of Tarpon Springs has made a number of overnight trips to the Middle Grounds, and he has advice for anyone making that long run offshore. He says some strange things can happen to boats offshore, often impossible to foresee, so it's best to prepare for a really bad experience, just in case.

"I strongly recommend carrying a satellite phone on such a trip; nothing works better if you get into trouble," he says. "Not cell phones; they won't have service that far offshore. The sat phones are more expensive, but they're getting cheaper."

that happens, they will probably be around the Marquesas instead. In the Park, you're only allowed a one-day bag limit while inside the anchorage, so you would want to visit there the first night, not the second. In the sheltered harbor, however, you can snorkel during the day and rest at night.

"The farther west you go away from the Keys, the less sophisticated the fish become," he says. "We don't need light tackle and lots of

Proper
Paperwork

Anglers visiting The Bahamas should realize they're guests in another country, which has different fishing laws entirely. Entry fees and paperwork are part of the regimen. Boats are required to show yellow quarantine flags until they've checked in through customs. Pay attention to Bahamian fish limits. Before heading out to the Islands, check for changes in customs or immigration laws at www.bahamas.com or call 1-800-32-SPORT. SB

To save fishing time, it's best to have the bulk of your paperwork done prior to arriving in The Bahamas.

Making the long runs means being with nature when the crowds are gone. Below, these runs often result in a really exotic mix of bottom fish.

T-top in groups of three," he says. "One person can pull them down and hand them out. I always bring extra drinking water, far more than can be consumed on the trip itself. If you get into trouble, you will need water.

"Always make sure that your bilge pumps work well before leaving the dock. Check your hull and any thru-hull fittings. Hoses under the deck are mostly attached with hose clamps that can rust. While spending the night offshore, I'm convinced you're better off leaving the bait pump turned off, and maybe putting any live bait in a net overboard. You don't want water pumping into the boat all night while people sleep; it's not a good idea.

"Check and double-check the weather before you go offshore on a long run. Postpone the trip if the weather is in question. Make the run in two boats, and fish with friends nearby, *especially* if you have a single engine boat. It's a long haul out there. Be sure your marine radio works well and was properly soldered to the antenna wire when installed. Another handy item is a hand-held radio that can be submerged. If you're left in the water, they can find you a lot easier. These have a range of one to three miles. Make sure the battery is good. With EPIRBS, if you have

McMillan says there are a variety of items you can carry offshore that would be handy in a bind. Some are even functional in the boat. Leisure seating floats are cushy, foam seats that can be slept on, rode on, and happen to be great to float on. A life raft is great, but if the CO_2 doesn't work, or time is required to self-inflate, you may not have the life raft if trouble happens fast. The foam seats work instantly. Guys have had to hang on to their ice chests while floating around, for lack of something better, and that's no fun.

"For life vests, I bundle them in the boat's

one, get it tested on a regular basis. They're floating distress buoys monitored by satellite, that are relayed to the Coast Guard.

Bigger boats even carry single-sideband radio, which has a range spanning the Gulf of Mexico. If you get a few of these safety items, you're so much better off than with nothing.

BE PREPARED FOR ANYTHING

"If you fish in winter far offshore, you can get hypothermia quickly," McMillan continued. "I stopped making the long runs in winter because it doesn't seem worth it. As for night fishing, there is lots of junk in the water, and if you run around at night you can hit something and knock a hole in the boat. Consider anchoring up at sunset, or moving around slowly at night. Also, be sure you have good lighting on your boat! Not just running lights, but mounted deck lights. And don't forget a four battery dive light or two, something sturdy, waterproof and powerful that will illuminate nearby boats or maybe navigation towers back inshore.

"A first aid kit should be on board. What if someone gets a hook in the hand? Learn some techniques on how to remove hooks from people. Keep a tool around that will cut through hooks. My favorite is a multi-purpose tool made by Braid Products, and it cuts a thick hook pretty well, even big treble hooks on trolling plugs. It's a great little tool. Another handy item is a pair of game shears, to cut bait and line. They easily cut braided line.

"If you plan the weather right, you can fish the Middle Grounds. To play it safe, I would recommend at least a 25-foot catamaran boat. With mono hulls, at least 28 feet. If you're a big risk-taker, people have made it out there in 20-footers and returned. For a much more comfortable ride, you'll need a 33-footer and up. Remember, the bigger boats cause a lot less stress on your back and body. Small boats can really take it out of you. If you're caught in rough seas in a smaller boat, ride in the back of the boat.

"I've been caught out there in really rough seas, and it isn't fun. We got caught at the Middle Grounds in August, and it actually got cold. Seas were 12 feet. Our boat fell into a deep hole between two big waves that was unbelievable. Everybody hit the deck, hard. My head hit the T-top. It's amazing the boat held together and nobody was hurt. Out of 25 to 30 trips to the Middle Grounds, eight or 10 were pretty trying times. Then you hit a flat trip, completely calm and wonderful, and I've had 3 to 5 trips like that.

"The hard-core commercial fishermen who have been going out there for 40 years say the Middle Grounds are just not meant for small boats, and not worth the hassle. Other areas

There's no better feeling than crossing deep ocean water in your own boat and catching exotic snapper and grouper.

A run to The Bahamas paid off for this South Florida angler.

inshore of there have good grouper fishing. Fishing the Middle Grounds can be just as tough as anywhere else; people get stuck fishing one way on the better-known spots and wonder where the grouper are. But any place that's a little difficult to find, and not getting dived or speared, is usually great. That's where the grouper will rise up and grab your baits

new at this, try to cross with another boat.

Other times of the year, you might get stuck in The Bahamas for days or weeks, waiting for decent weather to return. In bad enough weather, you may find seas in the Florida Straits from 15 to 20 feet high.

"Crossing is certainly safer than it used to be," Panos says. "Weather forecasts are better. NOAA weather on VHF radio reaches from Florida into the western Bahamas. The radio channels differ up and down the coast, but Channel 1 is used off Miami. Today's radar is much more widely used, even on the Internet, and that is great for

"We cross from Miami and stay at Bimini, Chub, Boat Harbor or Walker's Cay."

long before they reach bottom."

Crossing over to The Bahamas has been popular for many years, with some real adventures made by the public. It offers incredible scenery, deep water only a few yards offshore, and grouper and snapper paradise.

Capt. Dean Panos of Miami makes the crossing on a regular basis. He advises that anglers should make their crossings in summer when the weather is calmer. Peak visiting times are during full moons from May through July. That's when anglers are mostly after spawning mutton snapper. The afternoon summer squalls can get pretty strong, so it's best to cross first thing in the morning. If a problem arises, you have extra daylight hours to fix the problem or seek assistance. You wouldn't want to start across late in the day, without plenty of experience in local waters. He says if you're

Many high-tech mono hulls with twin engines as well as catamaran hulls are making longer runs offshore today.

detecting thunderstorms.

"For safety features, an EPIRB is almost mandatory. The offshore (yoke) style of life jackets should be on each vessel. Don't forget flares and the usual safety gear. Twin engines are better on each boat of course. Leave a float plan with someone dependable, showing where you plan to go, and stating when you expect to return. Keep in mind that fuel is at least $3 to $4 a gallon over there. Most fishing boats today are built with bigger fuel tanks than years ago, so they can fish around over there for three days without refueling.

"We commonly cross from Miami and stay at Bimini, Chub, Boat Harbor or Walker's Cay. The fishing is still very good. The Bahamas are a very large chain of islands, and commercial harvest is pretty light, except around bigger population centers. If there are fish traps around, we move off a few miles. They won't affect the yellowtail or mutton snapper, but they do affect grouper. The worst harvest problem I see is American boats keeping too many fish.

"Fishing over there means getting familiar with the place. I wouldn't advise someone to run around in the boat at night without local experience. Some ports are easier than others to enter at night, without hitting an underwater obstruction. Walker's can be tricky at night, for instance. I stopped fishing at night because I can catch as many fish in the daytime. I think the afternoon light from 3 to 7 p.m. is best for mutton snapper, anyway.

"Try the trip with friends in a second boat, and have fun. Keep in mind that rental rooms are scarce during summer in the Islands."

Also remember that The Bahamas is a sovereign nation with its own laws. SB

CHAPTER 14

Reef Trolling

Trolling for snapper and grouper has always been practical in shallow, coral reef waters, but modern advances in diving plug designs made it easier in slightly deeper water. Today, a family out trolling for the weekend, with minimal fishing experience offshore, can tie on a few plugs and pull them behind the boat in murky water up to 50 feet deep, catching sizeable grouper without even possessing secret spot "numbers" normally required for such a catch. On a broad area of live bottom, fully known to the fishing public, you can troll back and forth, picking off grouper up to 15 pounds and more. Even small kids can reel in these fish, since the boat helps pull them away from rocky cover.

Deep-diving plugs behind the boat really do catch snapper and grouper.

Tropical mutton snapper like the one above don't mind chasing after trolled plugs. Some plugs easily dive to 30 feet and more.

Trolling for Bottom Fish

Bottom fishermen are sometimes shocked to learn that in some regions of Florida's Gulf Coast, and even on the Atlantic side, anglers actually troll for grouper and snapper. The technique also works in The Bahamas and Caribbean. It requires a local population of bottom fish in less than 50 feet of water, fish that don't mind chasing deep-diving plugs that venture through their neighborhood. The lone exception is the free-ranging black grouper, a fish that will rise a hundred feet and more to smash at trolled artificial baits passing by on the surface.

PLUGS

Along more shallow stretches of Florida's Gulf, centered perhaps around the coastal bend where the Suwannee River meets salt water, grouper fishermen are very familiar with trolling plugs. These guys have caught limits of fine gag grouper while simply trolling over live bottom. The trick was more difficult before the advent of today's modern deep-diving plugs. A few years ago, the popular brands only wiggled down a dozen feet or so. If the water was 25 feet or less, feisty gags in the mood for a sardine meal didn't mind rising up a few feet to nail a passing Rapala, MirrOlure or Rebel Jawbreaker.

Today, trolling is easier, with plugs available with bigger lips, that dive two or three times the range of previous plugs. The Mann's Stretch 25 (the number denotes depth) was something of a pioneer, and when the Stretch 30 came out in the later 1990s, produced in myriad colors, Gulf boats soon had them sprouting from many rodtips. With a corresponding rise in popularity of bottom trolling, the locals soon saw new models in the marinas, such as the Yo-Zuri HydroMagnum DD and MirrOlure 25+. Mann's Stretch even came out with super models that dive to 40 and 50 feet, though both are quite large. There seems to be a barrier of sorts in delivering a free-swimming plug deeper than 40 feet. That currently requires a bigger plug, unless you attach a

When traveling to the Caribbean or The Bahamas, bring at least one trolling rod.

A happy guide in Belize smiles over a black grouper, caught in 18 feet of water with an older plug.

Some of the latest deeper-diving plugs include (l-r) MirrOlure 25+, Mann's Stretch 30, and Yo-Zuri Hydro Magnum.

Skirts rigged with ballyhoo certainly catch black grouper.

lead weight beneath the lip, like the Yo-Zuri.

One of the fun parts of grouper trolling along this stretch of the Florida coast is never knowing what will hit next. Seabass of a pound and more are common bycatch, as they'll attack baits bigger than themselves. Catching a dozen seabass makes for a fine meal, since they're delicious. A big kingfish or Spanish mackerel will often take a shot at these diving plugs, too. Even oddball fish; one Suwannee angler had a 7-pound flounder attack his trolled, Stretch 30 plug in almost 40 feet of water offshore. He must have grabbed that plug very close to the bottom.

The trick to getting the most from a trolled plug is to use braided line (or less sporting wire) that is so much thinner than monofilament. The plug just goes deeper. On one test using similar Stretch 30s, a black and silver model with 30-pound braided line caught 17 gag grouper in just one day, while the blue and silver model, pulled with 40-pound mono

line, had one strike with the fish lost. Braided line pulled through rod guides that aren't super-smooth will ultimately fray with continued use, so roller guides on the rods aren't a bad idea. A roller tip is advisable, anyway. Also, ceramic rod guides seem to work better than stainless steel guides.

Around St. Marks near Tallahassee, and the Yankeetown-Crystal River area southeast of Suwannee, shallow water and rocks only a few feet beneath the surface are home to gag grouper. The trolling plugs in those regions are not so big-lipped. Some may have the older models that dive a dozen feet, or they may have tiny lips that keep them only a foot or two beneath the surface. The trick here is to avoid snagging bottom all day, but position the plug within range of hungry gags.

Groupers will hit repeatedly at trolled plugs, and it isn't uncommon to hook two fish at

once. Two of these fish, hooked together, put a terrific stress on the plug, sometimes ripping out the stainless steel split rings attached to treble hooks. Big treble hooks may be com-

Grouper will hit repeatedly at trolled plugs, and it isn't uncommon to hook two fish at once.

pletely ripped from the plugs. At least the plug can be repaired later.

One need not use expensive tackle for grouper trolling. Older reels with sturdy rods are fine. And, when traveling in The Bahamas or Caribbean, it pays to bring along at least one rod and reel with 40- or 50-pound line. Even a few minutes of pulling plugs around nearby coral reefs can spice up the day and catch something for dinner, either grouper, snapper or perhaps a barracuda.

The tropical mutton snapper doesn't mind chasing after trolled plugs. In the Florida Keys, some boaters have trolled up and down the seven-mile bridge near Marathon, catching a mix of snapper and grouper. When a fish is hooked, the boat is abruptly turned 90 degrees away from the bridge, pulling the fish away from structure. On the coral reefs, towing big-lipped plugs past coral heads and through submerged canyons may also produce a mix of muttons and black grouper.

In the Caribbean and The Bahamas, muttons are the obvious target snapper for trollers, using skirted ballyhoo on the shallow grassflats surrounding the patch reefs. Cubera snapper also hit trolled plugs; the Belize River and various deep creeks are favorites for these fish, which live beneath undercut banks. Other cuberas are caught off the reefs. Black and some yellowfin are the groupers most frequently targeted on island reefs by trollers, especially in winter, when these fish move into shallow water. (See chapter on black grouper.) In addition, yellowtail snapper will readily hit small jigs, rigged ballyhoo and smaller lipped plugs when trolling.

One caution when using trolling plugs: the

treble hooks are sharp, large diameter, sometimes loose and flailing, and an angry grouper
can whip a hook into your hand faster than
the eye can follow. For hook removal from
fish, use gloves and a long pair of needlenose
pliers. Sometimes, it's best to cut the line and
store the entire rig with fish in the ice chest,
until the grouper settles down.

DOWNRIGGERS

Pulling live baits near bottom will also catch
snapper and grouper. Sometimes the bait must
remain a good ways behind the "cannon ball"
weight, an unfamiliar object that can spook
some fish. On a hot bite or a new spot, gag
grouper to 15 pounds will chase after live, 8-
inch blue runners trolled near bottom. In
Tampa Bay anglers do just that using downrig-
gers. The main ship channel there, with its
deep dropoffs and huge bridge, makes that bay
the best in Florida and no doubt the country,
for trolling up a limit of grouper.

PLANERS

Though more complicated, a flat, metal
planer will deliver a bait deep, with perhaps a
plug, spoon or belly strip of cut bait as an
offering to bottom fish. When a fish hits, the
planer is "tripped" and stops digging water,
where it becomes a mere attachment out in
front of the leader. The fish is then reeled up.

TRAILERS

These are unweighted
flies, really just a hank of
hair or Mylar material,
wrapped around a strong,
4/0 hook. Using three or
more feet of mono leader,
they can be tied to the
back of a trolling plug,
trailing behind. It is the
plug that delivers the fly
deep enough for fish to
attack. On some days,
grouper will hit the fly,
more so than the plug.
Unruly seabass will hit the
fly over and over, sometimes to a fault, but the
end result is often enough fish for a fine meal.

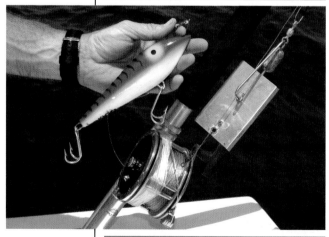

Above: adjusting downrigger while trolling for
grouper in Tampa Bay. Blue runner as live bait.
Bottom: Reel with wire line, metal planer, dive plug.

Mutton snapper are fond of artificial baits. Many
have been caught by trollers in the Florida Keys,
near coral reefs and long bridges in deeper water.

CHAPTER 15

Deep Dropping

Deep-drop fishing doesn't appeal to everyone, because it's tough and many people aren't that good at it. By dropping deep we mean *really* deep, as in 500 to 1,500 feet of water, where conventional tackle can be used, but is impractical.

"If I find a good piece of bottom and pull up one good fish, it's great," says Capt. George LaBonte, who fishes out of Jupiter, Florida. "I find appeal in the technical demands, getting baits that deep, finding a patch of bottom or a sunken wreck so remote. Deploying a bait and hitting the spot just right. You're certainly pushing harder than anchoring over a shallow reef for yellowtails. This is *extreme* bottom fishing."

The Bahamas are the ideal venue because land is near, and the currents are slow except near Bimini.

Fifty-pound snowy grouper reeled up from 900 feet with 50-wide manual reel. Catch two or three of these guys, and you won't have much room left in the fishbox.

Anglers fishing in the Gulf of Mexico obviously have to venture far offshore for dropping baits deep, except along the Western Panhandle. Generally, the close dropoffs have been hit hardest by fishermen. Venture out a hundred miles to some shelf,

Queen snapper brought up from 1,000 feet. Below, snowy grouper from 900.

however, and the fish are far more numerous and receptive. The narrow bottom off West Palm Beach, for instance, is fished hard. More distant ledges in Northeast Florida see far less pressure. Atlantic anglers must deal with the powerful Gulf Stream current, which is so

strong on some days, it completely protects the fish from passing hooks. All coastal states offer deepwater snapper and grouper action; you just have to get out there with the right stuff, meaning gear. What sorts of fish are out there in deeper water along or off the continental shelf? Much of it is still unknown.

The Bahamas are the ideal venue for deep-dropping, because currents there are slow except near Bimini. And there are so many deepwater spots within easy sight of land. "The Bahamas are best," LaBonte says. "You can really work a small area, a house-sized target 1,500 feet down, because of the lack of current. That's where people focus on small yelloweye snapper," says LaBonte. "But there are tons of stuff out deeper, beyond 900 and out to 2,000 feet. We get queen snapper up to 20 pounds, wenchman (my personal favorite to eat) up to 6 to 7 pounds, big yelloweye (silk snapper) to 10 pounds, and then maybe something no one has ever seen. You spend enough time out there, you'll catch something that *nobody* can find in a book.

"In the Florida Keys, it can still be pretty good out there," he says. "The fish are there. Most people aren't really good at deep dropping, and it's a lot of work. You need to have the interest and then really get into it. There are good yelloweye snapper in the Keys, which we seldom see up north off Jupiter. Even at the Hump off Islamorada, off the edge in 400 to 500 feet, people are catching yelloweyes. That's a good place to start. Out in deeper water, there's Wood's Wall down in the Lower Keys where the billfish boats go. Any structure down there will have something swimming around."

Tossing out the lead stick with baited hooks for silk snapper, in 400 feet. Baits are kept small to match the snapper in that depth zone.

A doubleheader of silk snapper, reeled up with the help of electric tackle. Without it, pulling up these fish can turn into a real grind.

Deep and Deeper

For bait, a lot of guys go with skin fish, which is anything with a tough skin. Favorite skin baits in South Florida and The Bahamas are bonito and barracuda, easy to acquire by trolling. Elsewhere, it might be blue runner and blackfin tuna. Squid gets cleaned off the hook, if you don't match the hook size with the right kind of fish down there. That's a pain, having to reel up empty hooks from 900 feet. But squid is still very effective. Use two rods at the same time, and the rod with squid will get more bites. Little blackfin snappers only 6 to 7 inches long can swarm the baits and steal them. If this happens, put on only enough cut squid to cover the hook, and don't leave much extra hanging off the hook for something to tug on.

Sash weights are the cheap option for fishing deep, the iron weights salvaged from older

Tackle is heavy: "There are beasts down

Bottom rig ready to go deep. Sturdy cut bait with skin attached is most popular, followed by squid.

homes. If you use one, wrap it with duct tape. Ultimately, most anglers end up buying lead sticks. "I carry every size of weight from 2 to 12 pounds," says LaBonte. "Be sure when attaching the weight to use a breakaway line. If you snag bottom, it's usually the weight that hangs up. Use 80-pound wire or line that will break way before the main leader might. Wire the weight to a large snap swivel. Watch for line frays around the weight, because it can get banged up, drifting across rocky bottom."

As for the leader, no less than 200-pound mono should be used, with an upward range of 400- or 500-pound leader. Sturdy, 3-way swivels are advised. Crimps are mandatory, instead of knots. Some main leaders are made of wire, when sharks are around. The hook drops are mono, so the shark has a chance of

Silk snapper brought up from 400 feet. Below, young anglers watch the depths expectantly, hoping to see red-colored fish on the way up.

there that can take everything."

biting through one, preventing a long battle. "There are beasts down there that take everything," says LaBonte. Some big sharks live on the bottom, while others, such as oceanic whitetips, will intercept your fish on the way up. That is especially true in The Bahamas. All you can do is bring your fish up fast, and keep 'em coming. You're limited on the speed of the reel, so keep your finger on the button.

Hooks should match the fish in the area. Fish that have a small mouth—generally less than 10 pounds—require a small hook. Small yelloweye and blackfin snappers are a good example. If you have bigger hooks and want bigger fish, move offshore into deeper water. "My snapper rig has 13/0 circle hooks," LaBonte says. "I go as big as 16/0. I used to target bigger fish, but they're not that great to eat.

Ready made bottom rigs with glow in the dark dropper rigs, with six circle hooks, are inexpensive to buy but are very much worth it. These days, if I'm in The Bahamas, I go for queen and yelloweye (silk) snapper. To keep a string of circle hooks straight, you can drive around with the rod in one holder, and the sinker across the deck in another holder. Other guys just keep everything in a bucket. That way, the baits don't drip on the deck. A 200- or 300-pound leader isn't going to get kinked up in a bucket. It might take a moment to untangle, though."

The rewards of deep-dropping can be great. LaBonte has caught strings of fish on his six circle hook rigs, sometimes more in one drop than other boats catch in a long day of fishing, back inshore. "My biggest warsaw weighed about 250 pounds, and we get misty grouper from 60 to 70 pounds. Wreckfish are deeper, sometimes 1,800 feet down, weighing from 50 to 100 pounds. Where I fish, the snowy grouper aren't too big (like they are off Texas and Louisiana) but we do get tasty tilefish as big as 25 to 30 pounds. That's a real kick." SB

Dragged up from the Deep

Yellowedge grouper caught in 720 feet. More common in the western Gulf of Mexico, they grow to about 30 pounds. This one was caught on a 50-pound class reel without electrics. Anglers trolling for tuna near an oil rig simply stopped, rigged a trolling rod with two circle hooks, chunks of blackfin tuna and a big sash weight, and dropped it down.

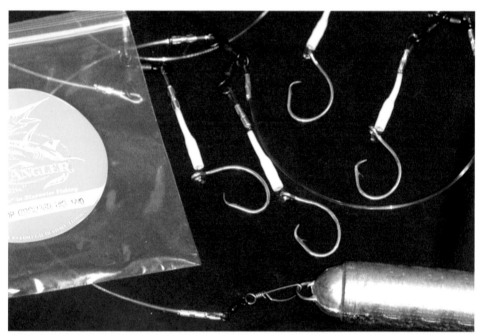

Tools of the trade. Above, a pre-packaged bottom rig properly made for deep-dropping. Cut baits below are being prepared for the hooks. The most popular cut baits are tough and have a thick skin, to better stay on the hook. Favorite local fish for cut baits include barracuda, little tunny, blackfin tuna, blue runners, and various members of the jack family, including this crevalle jack. If large grouper are present, simply use bigger chunks, cut in streamlined shapes that will cause less drag in the water. The other bait alternative is to use frozen squid, which don't stay on the hook as well, but are favored by all deepwater bottom species, since squid are so abundant in all areas.

What sort of bottom?

Anglers are often curious what sort of bottom is down there in the deeper depths, that would attract species of snapper and grouper new to them. Places that no diver has ever seen. What should anglers really be looking for?

"Anything out of the ordinary," says Capt.

George LaBonte. "There are lots of ledges parallel to the coastline. A little patch of hard bottom, a wreck, whatever. It's the same as fishing shallow water, you look for something different that attracts fish, since there is mostly sand or mud desert all around."

You can actually mark fish that far down. It takes a powerful bottom machine with a good transducer. Start with a 1,000 kilowatt machine with a good, thru-the-hull transducer. "That's key to finding bottom while moving around with the boat. Any bubbles will look like static and mess up the picture," he said.

It's quite dark 1,000 feet below the surface, unless the water is very calm and it's high noon and cloudless that day. Most deep-drop anglers now use lights attached to the top of their leaders. "Deep-droppers have a saying: 'No light, no bite,'" says LaBonte. "Lights have become standard on our leaders. They're battery-powered."

Four or five companies make suitable deep-drop lights, with tackle catalogs and shops slowly picking up on the growing market.

"Forget chemical light sticks; they implode below about 300 feet," says LaBonte. They'll stay on the line, but they always return empty of fluids and light. Quality bottom lights cost about $40 each. You attach them to the leader, and they're a real incentive not to get hung up on rocky bottom. They either flash a strobe, or remain on. SB

Deep-droppers have a saying: no light, no bite. That's because it's mostly dark so far below, even at high noon. Most popular light for this job is a combination of blue and green.

Pair of snowy grouper reeled up from 900 feet with conventional reel and 50-pound mono line! Smaller fish did not inflate from pressure.

CHAPTER 16

Conservation

Conservation of marine resources takes many forms. It requiries an attitude that we should be leaving fish out there for tomorrow's generation. This idea is admittedly foreign to many people. That's why we have fishery laws, to remedy a host of modern problems that have manifested in various fisheries: Overly efficient gear, advances in electronics, lax limits, too many people on a fishery, fishermen camping on spawning aggregations—almost all fishermen make their impacts, large or small.

Ethics is the key issue. Fishermen can only study the conservation issues, spread the word, and try to treat the resource with more respect.

Conservation ethics include simple things like changing techniques or moving on, if only small fish are being caught and thrown back.

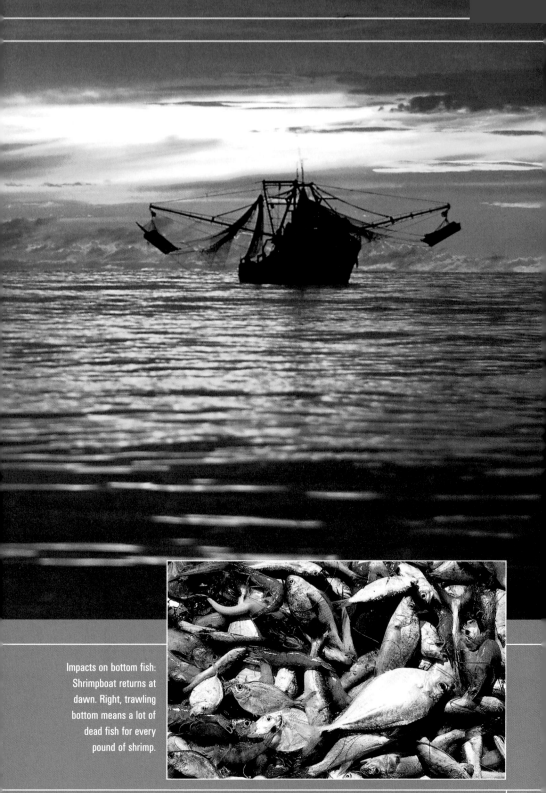

Impacts on bottom fish: Shrimpboat returns at dawn. Right, trawling bottom means a lot of dead fish for every pound of shrimp.

Ethical Considerations

Conservation covers a number of items large and small that impact fish populations. A simple pair of needlenose pliers, for instance, may directly affect a fish's survival if it means the hook was removed cleanly. Compared against the thousand-pound hauls of a 60-foot grouper longline boat the pliers aren't much, but both have a cumulative effect on grouper and snapper populations. There are lots of ways to conserve bottom fish.

For instance, fishermen should always take care to properly handle and release their undersized fish. With today's tight bag and size limits, there are lots of opportunities to do so, and this is an important skill every angler should learn. Landing fish in a timely manner before they're exhausted, handling them gently, backing the hook out without causing damage, and getting that fish back in the water quickly—these are important skills.

Camping out over small fish, hoping to catch a keeper or two, is not good conservation, for instance. Throwing back 50 "short" red grouper usually means a few of those fish won't survive, for one reason or another. Better to move on. It's the same with red snapper: If small fish are coming aboard in a steady fashion, try something else, perhaps bigger baits at mid-depth, where small snapper seldom go. It's the same with most bottom fish. Fish a little above bottom with bigger baits, or move on to another spot.

Some anglers on the Gulf side of Florida are still targeting fish with no bag limits. Abusing these rights later often requires changing the law, when another fish population begins to

Small red snapper now protected by size limits. Below, even hook selection has conservation impact.

crater. Seabass, grunts and sand trout are often hammered by anglers, many of them from out of state, folks hoping to stock their freezer with fillets.

Even the choice of hooks makes a difference on fish stocks. Circle hooks, for instance, are swallowed far less often than any other variety. Stainless steel hooks last for at least a few years in salt water, a danger to everything that encounters them. Lost treble hooks may actually lock a fish's jaws shut, or render it unable to swallow. And, barbless hooks are more easily removed from fish, causing less damage. So, conservation choices are made even while shopping for tackle.

Huge goliath grouper were speared commercially for many years, until earning protection in 1990.

The conscientious bottom fisherman carries a few items while on the water, to ensure a better survival rate of released fish.

VENTING YOUR CATCH

While shopping for tackle, one should include a vent needle for releasing undersized bottom fish. Or bigger fish, for that matter. Taking a little care to reel up a snapper or

grouper slowly, and venting it properly, will help ensure the health of released fish. Vent needles are needed beyond depths of 100 feet, and that importance only increases beyond that depth. In 200 feet and beyond, every released bottom fish should be vented quickly. The gas inside these fish doubles for every 33 feet they're brought up. That's what scuba divers call getting "the bends," and it's fatal to fish as well. Common signs are an everted stomach, eyes bugging and scales ruptured. On the partyboats, some deckhands are quick to poke and release the undersized fish, using nothing more than the sharp point from a cheap cord fish stringer. (Just the right diameter.) Hollow steel tubes are better, of course.

HOOK REMOVERS

So-called "hookouts" are needed, to safely unhook fish for a quicker release. These are designed in different ways, often nothing more than a long pair of needle-nose pliers. They're meant for reaching far inside fish to dislodge the hook. The needlenose is necessary for unhooking large treble hooks used on trolling plugs. Reaching for a mouthful of treble hooks on a trolling plug, while still attached to a thrashing, angry grouper is almost a guaranteed ticket to a doctor's clinic. Keep several pairs of "hookouts" around the boat cockpit, or wear one on your belt. Some captains even spray-paint theirs red, so they can be spotted quickly in a crowded cockpit. If they're painted, they won't rust as quickly.

TOWELS AND GLOVES

A small, rough hand towel or a protective glove is handy when gripping a fish around the head or open gill plate. One shouldn't wrap up the entire fish with the towel, which removes protective slime. Wrapping a fish's head can be great for quieting them, after they land on deck. The towel also keeps hands clean while working in the boat. Slippery hands lose a number of rods overboard each year, when a big fish suddenly hits.

Gloves protect the hands, while at the same

Above, vent tool releases gas from red grouper. Middle, a "hookout" tool quickly unhooks a mutton snapper. Below, using a towel to handle Nassau grouper.

Save a Fish, Use a Camera

Photographing fish as proof of the catch means more fish may be released.

Even a camera can be a conservation tool, by snapping a few quick pictures before releasing a good-sized fish. Though big snapper and grouper aren't often released, in truth the biggest fish aren't so great on the table. If so, the picture itself may be worth far more than the fillets. This would especially be true if the fish was a large cubera snapper or black grouper, both of which have reputations for sometimes carrying ciguatera toxin. They pick it up by feeding for years along the coral reefs, and it accumulates. The bigger the predator fish, the more likely it may carry the toxin. Many anglers now consider a good picture of themselves with a 50-pound cubera to be the only feasible souvenir from the trip. Such a large fish (often caught in September during spawning duties) deserves to be released for two reasons: to continue spawning, and to avoid poisoning the angler. Thus the camera. SB

Charterboats

Conservation is an ongoing process

In some areas, charterboat captains still sell the day's catch, though the notion seems outdated in modern times. When tourists fly in for a few day's fishing, many of these fishermen are unable to haul fish back or ship them home, without some inconvenience. Many have no interest in hauling fish around. Some don't even eat fish. So, the fish end up on the dock, advertising for the next day's trip. That's how charterboat captains living on the coast, where living expenses may be high, are practically forced to sell their catch. The fish are on the dock—what to do with them next?

Charterboat crews have various incentives to make a good catch each day, and selling increasingly pricey fish is just one of them. Anglers who consider hiring charterboats should know that charterboat law doesn't require they dump their catch on the dock. It's legal to release fish. Despite the song and dance routine from some crew members, any bottom fish caught in 150 feet or less can be released, by venting the gas from these fish. Even an icepick or thin fillet knife will work. Often it's not even needed, if the fish is brought up slowly. One can check with a charterboat before booking, to see how interested they are in releasing fish. Especially bottom fish.

Releasing fish is easy and doesn't really hurt. Those photos taken while out on the boat last a lifetime.

At any rate, there's something not right about charterboats constantly selling their bottom fish, with or without a license, from their own port, fish that can easily be 20 years old. The numbers just don't add up. SB

Big warsaw grouper on a charterboat dock.

time allowing anglers to grab flopping fish on deck and release them without wasting time. On a long weekend of bottom fishing, including overnight trips and tournaments, gloves can make a difference in how efficiently the hands still function.

SCALES AND GRIPPERS

A pair of portable scales can also be a conservation tool. Weighing a fish that is short of some goal, like a tournament fish or a world record, ensures not killing it for a dockside weigh-in. For instance, if a 20-pound mutton snapper is leading the Miami MET Tournament, there may be reason to release slightly smaller fish. Tournament fishing is usually aimed at a certain weight bracket of fish, and releasing those that fall short helps ensure more fish are available the following year.

Gripping tools like the one pictured at far right make it easy and safe to hold up fish for a photo, perhaps before releasing them. Some have built-in scales, a very handy feature.

Conservation is an ongoing process that constantly requires fine-tuning. There wasn't much point in detailing the latest bag and size limits as this book was going to press, because books last a long time, and fisheries change. However, we have listed a number of practices later in this chapter, that have degraded snapper and grouper populations in the Atlantic and Gulf, along with solutions that have helped conserve these fish.

TAGGING

Tagging and releasing fish has the curious effect of showing anglers it doesn't really hurt to throw quality fish back in the water. It's like a lightbulb pops over an angler's head: Hey! Why have I been keeping so many fish for the freezer? I'm tired of eating old, frozen fish...

Some fishermen have even organized tag-

and-release tournaments, with a list of perhaps 10 priority fish species. Points are awarded for each, and the winner gets a donated prize and trophy of some kind. Data cards are filled out on every fish, with the usual length, weight and location, among other items. Anglers with the knowledge to catch a variety of local fish usually win these tournaments. The absence of cash or high-ticket prizes means that everyone stays honest. It's less of a competitive thing, everyone works for a good cause, and you don't see people with their "game faces" on before the event.

The end result is a pile of data cards, perhaps on some fish that have never been actively tagged before. Some of the fish recaptures are the only data that future researchers start out with, when they begin to investigate a species. Recaptures also show participating anglers how finite our marine resources are. The overlying idea seems to be, "Whoa, if I hadn't tagged and released that fish, Joe Shmo in the next state down the coast, wouldn't have caught a trophy fish that day..."

That has the effect of making fishermen realize what a small world we really live in.

Above, gripper tool safely holds up and weighs fish. Below, feisty gag grouper just tagged with no ill effects, about to be released in the Atlantic.

Destructive Fish Traps

Unfortunately, it's easy to fish with illegal traps. Buoys can stay submerged until Monday.

Fish traps became illegal on the Atlantic side of Florida in 1982. Ridding that entire coast of legal traps caused a real comeback of grouper and snapper, along with myriad tropical reef species. It was about time, too; fish trapping is incredibly wasteful on bottom fish. Hauled quickly to the surface by hydraulic winch, almost everything in the trap

diameter, as years of fish bones fell through or were pulled through by feeding crabs. The traps were estimated to have been lost for two to four years, with many more years of fishing still ahead of them. It's a continuous drain on the local reef fish population. Thousands of traps have been lost over the years, often when a hurricane passes through an area. Finding and disposing of them will not be easy.

Deeper traps in the Keys and Dry Tortugas have been filmed in almost 330 feet of water, many of them abandoned for years. Each had plenty of grouper inside, and lots of bones on the outside. Coupled with the realization that trapping has been going on since the 1970s with annual loss of this gear, especially after hurricanes, it makes one wonder what the real cost of traps has been. In some countries like Haiti, Dominica and Jamaica, it has been crippling. Traps have been called the cocaine of commercial fishing gear, because once fishermen begin using them, they won't use anything else, they can't stop, and it's very destructive.

Unfortunately, it's easy to fish with illegal traps. The buoys can be submerged, and rigged to surface on Mondays or Tuesdays, after the weekend crowd of recreational anglers has gone home. All it takes is a release device made with a small zinc anode, that decays in a set time while exposed to salt water. So, anglers who fish after the weekend should keep an "eye peeled," as sailors used to say, for small buoys that have surfaced in fishing areas, without the more common crab or lobster buoys scattered around in sight. For instance, if you're fishing over a wreck and a single, tiny buoy, perhaps painted a dark color, is bobbing on the surface, chances are it may be an illegal trap.

Boaters who find a trap are reminded that it is illegal to pull one, much less cut the buoy rope. That would only create another

Florida Marine Patrol picks up another string of illegal fish traps, fortunately in calm weather.

dies. It's really a Third World method of fishing, a phenomenon that has practically wiped out reef fish stocks in Jamaica and Haiti, for instance.

Lost or "ghost" traps continue to fish for many years after. Fish swim inside to feed on the dead fish that slowly starved. They in turn become food that attracts more fish. Submersibles have filmed abandoned traps with a neighboring "bone field" up to 20 feet in

Below, black grouper sulks in illegal fish trap found in Florida Keys. Above, illegal trap found off Louisiana.

ghost trap. One should write down the exact GPS number of the buoy, and then contact a marine enforcement officer. Illegal trappers may leave a scattering of small, dark, even half-buoys over live bottom, sometimes a hundred yards apart. In flat, calm seas, they can be spotted, especially when crab and lob-

ster season is over.

On the Gulf side of Florida, all fish traps were scheduled to be phased out by the year 2007. For years, traps were restricted to water 60 feet or deeper. But shallow-water traps, marked with innocuous stone crab buoys, have been illegally worked for years off

Florida's Big Bend. Steinhatchee in particular was a problem area. Once-numerous seabass and grunts in the area became more scarce during the hey-day of illegal trapping. The traps also contained lots of small grouper. Key arrests were finally made by state officers, who pulled traps and injected fish with computer data chips. Computer-coded fish were detected at the local fishhouse, hard evidence that the same fish came from illegal, inshore traps with known GPS coordinates. Arrests were made and 2,216 pounds of grouper, seabass and grunts were confiscated from just one commercial boat.

So, it's easy to see how much damage this one method of capture can cause.

BOTTOM LONGLINES

They are frequently used for grouper and snapper, and they've taken millions of pounds. They can target the spawning stock of large red snapper, by setting over likely bottom in 200 to 300 feet. (That's where many 20-plus-pound red snapper are caught.) Longliners also take more than 90 percent of deepwater grouper, mostly snowy, warsaw and yellowedge. And they've taken the bulk of red grouper catches off the west coast of Florida, because these fish spread out across miles of live but fairly flat bottom.

Bottom longlines sometimes utilize miles of line across the bottom, and with lots of circle hooks. In 1990, they were outlawed inshore of

The Price of Shrimp For every pound of shrimp, from

Shrimpboats alone have caused amazing damage to the Gulf's red snapper fishery. It is an unfortunate fact that tiny red snapper are fond of the same soft Gulf bottom frequented by shrimp. The result has been millions of small red snapper wasted every year since the advent of Gulf shrimping. Some 7,000 shrimpboats prowled the Gulf at one time, dragging endlessly, though that number is far fewer today. Imported shrimp has dropped the overall price, while the price of diesel and everything else has gone up.

For every pound of shrimp, from three to 20 pounds of fish are caught and wasted. Offshore anglers who stop around the shrimpboats have often seen the heaps of "deck trash" on deck—unfortunately made up of many species of marine life, including red snapper. On a calm and glassy day, this cargo is shoveled overboard and can be readily identified or even retrieved by small boat. Thousands of snapper, sand trout and croakers can be spotted floating behind a single shrimpboat, and all three species have been adversely impacted in the last 30 years by shrimping. (Of the three, snapper have been improving, but only after seasonal closures and very tight bag limits). Special bycatch reduction devices have been installed on shrimpnets in many areas, but it remains to be seen if they will solve the problem. SB

120 feet in many areas. Experts argue that longlines should be made illegal altogether.

It doesn't take many longline boats to land millions of pounds of grouper. For instance, from 1990 to 1998, Florida's longline boats landed an average of 2.8 million pounds of red grouper each year. During that last year of the survey, there were 181 longline boats working offshore. During that same period, commercial boats landed 87 percent of all red grouper, with 60 percent of those boats being longliners. So, maintaining a healthy fishery for grouper of any kind clearly means regulating longline

Circle hook used for bottom longlines is very efficient.

fishermen in an appropriate way.

Bandit fishing is also called "vertical fishing," as in dropping baits straight down. It's a more old-fashioned method, though about 15 circle hooks can be used, with a 5- to 10-pound weight. The rig is called bandit fishing

three to 20 pounds of fish are caught and wasted.

Shrimpboat plies the Gulf of Mexico. Thousands of these boats stayed offshore for weeks at a time, impacting fish and marine life.

Red snapper speared by diver. Anglers complain about spearfishermen, another user conflict.

the Atlantic seaboard with the seasons, working Florida reefs each winter, and then moving up as far as North Carolina each summer. With advanced gas mixes, they're working in deeper and deeper water. Wrecks in 200 feet can be worked over and relieved of their bigger snapper and grouper, perhaps leaving the amberjack. This doesn't make area fishermen very happy, and it's just one more example of user conflict. Meanwhile, it's important that recreational anglers desist from selling their catch, like they did in the old days.

As an example, in August of 1975, a spear fisherman snorkeled out from Destin beach, out to the end of the west jetty, shooting the only two gag groupers in the neighborhood, a pair of 12-pounders. After being cautioned about numerous sharks in the area from a nearby boat, he accepted an offer for a safe ride back to the beach. (Some healthy sharks were spotted while en route). He sold the groupers to a fish market right next to the big bridge overlooking the pass. It seems that the tourist needed money for a motel room that very night. That spear fisherman today is the editor of this book, and his road trip from Texas to Destin that summer in a Volkswagen was just the sort of thing people did back then. (Some people, anyway). Visiting Florida and extending the vacation by selling fish has a long tradition, but is no longer acceptable. Too many people, not enough fish. This law is just one way of controlling landings of bottom fish.

Commercial spearfishing still exists and has expanded. In some areas it's common during summer. The divers use "powerheads," hitting fish underwater with a bullet of some kind, which is fatal to the fish. Some divers imported from other countries can easily snorkel dive to 50 feet and more, and the fish can't hear them approaching, since "free divers" are silent compared against scuba divers, who leave a bubble trail. Charter captains report that many of the shallower Gulf wrecks are virtually

perhaps because the contraption has one arm on the side, often for manual cranking, which is reminiscent of the old "one-armed bandits," which are gambling (slot) machines.

During the same survey period in 1998, some 1,207 "bandit" or vertical fishing commercial boats landed 1.1 million pounds of red grouper in Florida. These very same vessels can fish in deeper water for other species of grouper and snapper, and often do, but they're relegated to anchoring, or drift-fishing when the current is slow enough. Red grouper spread out well, favoring small holes and live bottom, including sponges, so vertical fishing doesn't impact them nearly as much as longlining.

SPEARFISHING

Commercial spearfishing doesn't get much press, but there are people who make money spearing fish and selling snapper and grouper. This is a gray area, because recreational divers who spear fish remain sport divers, unless they sell their catch. In years past, there were few laws and anyone could unload their catch at the local fish market to pay for their trip offshore. Today, a commercial license is required to sell any fish. That means folks who sell their catch are commercial fishermen. Or carry a commercial license, anyway. They may be doctors or lawyers, but they've obtained a license to sell their fish.

Some spearfishermen migrate up and down

cleaned out by spear fishermen when the water warms enough to dive each spring.

Fishing and diving the same spot invariably spooks bottom fish, so fishermen and divers have a tenuous relationship when anchored close by. Gag grouper, a smart species as fish go, are quick to vacate the area when spears begin flying. On many spots they leave while divers are still approaching. Mutton snapper are the same way. Most grouper and snapper in fact stop feeding when divers around them show intent to harm. This doesn't bode well for fishermen anchored above.

Spear fishermen tend to target the biggest bottom fish they can get in their sights. Many goliath grouper were taken in this way, sometimes slaughtered by the dozen at certain wrecks that hosted spawning aggregations, to the point where that species had to be protected from all capture in 1990. Spear fishermen have only switched to other fish, with large, male black and gag grouper being a real prize. Shooting (and sometimes only wounding) the top reef predators on a wreck or reef is seldom a good idea from a reproductive standpoint, especially large, male grouper. It doesn't make much sense, but many divers armed with spearguns have a hard time resisting a macho shot or marketing their fish.

Prior to 1980, shallow waters in the Florida Keys held black grouper and lots of mangrove

Size Limits Fish should contribute at least once to the gene pool.

Size limits are implemented after research by biologists, usually predicated on the minimum size at which a certain species begins spawning. They feel a fish should contribute at least once to the gene pool, before being exposed to legal capture. If fishing pressure keeps growing on legal fish, then bumping up the minimum size by an inch or two protects a great many more fish. For instance, many thousands of "short" red grouper are caught

Angler measures his red snapper for legal status.

each year off Florida's west coast, respectable, barrel-bodied fish that aren't quite of legal size. The result has been lots of fishing action, with some captains complaining that these fish eat up all of their bait, and still have to be released. The result will likely be a great many more, keeper-sized red grouper in that area.

Bag limits are geared toward maintaining an adequate stock of spawning fish each year. If stocks fall, fishermen are regulated by bag limits. However, there is a fine line. If bag limits are too drastic, anglers stop pursuing certain species, and the coastal fishing economy (boat building, charterboats, marinas, tackle industry, bait catchers) all suffer.

When fishing pressure was much lighter, and far fewer boats could be found offshore, there were no bag or even size limits on any bottom fish at all. Folks could keep whatever they caught, and sell their catch. It took a long time, but stocks of grouper and snapper were finally brought down to where strict fisheries management was needed to protect future stocks.

That's why we have fishery laws. And lots of conservation issues to deal with. SB

Huge "copperbelly" male gag grouper are much in demand for spawning duties in the Gulf of Mexico.

Indeed, overfishing in the snapper-grouper fishery reached crisis levels in the 1980s, mainly due to fish traps, longlines, hydraulic rigs and poor quota management. Limits for personal-use fishing also were weak.

Better management, however, has resulted in major rebounds for bottom-fish populations. It's clear that traditional laws regarding gear and limits can keep fish populations high without resorting to draconian lockouts of the general public.

Our position is that it's far better for the public to manage the fish properly everywhere rather than to impose drastic no-fish-

snapper, among others, that could be pursued all day with snorkel gear in only 10 feet of water. Then the action dried up. Folks blamed commercial spear fishermen, and many of the fish brought in were in fact sold to fish markets in the Keys and back in Miami. The result was a gradual disappearance (compared with former years) of most of these fish in such shallow waters.

NO-FISHING ZONES

In an effort to stop commercial fishing excesses that have depleted dozens of fisheries, some groups have been pushing for the creation of huge no-fishing zones that ban not just commercial overkills but family-level fishing as well.

Now called marine reserves, these no-fishing zones have been promoted by some for two decades.

Sponge Boats

Why sponges are still harvested in Florida waters is a mystery, when you consider what critical habitat they provide for young lobsters, shrimp, fish, octopus and many other animals.

Reef material and even sea fans in the Keys carry a heavy price if someone is caught with even one of them, yet sponges are still fair game for anyone with a license to harvest seafood. Protected by the Feds in Everglades National Park, who say sponges are a vital component of marine bay systems, sponges still remain a marketable catch in most of Florida's coastal waters.

Sponges attach to flat, hard bottom (thus the name "live" bottom) and they can be the tallest structure for miles around. Red grouper on Florida's west coast in particular use them for cover, while waiting for dinner to pass by.

As for water quality, it's been said that a one-gallon sponge can filter and clean enough seawater daily to fill a small, backyard swimming pool. Clean the sponges out, and water quality declines. It's that simple. A sponge's primary food source is tiny algae, bacteria and various organic particles in seawater, and they

ing edicts in a few chosen areas while over-fishing continues outside zone boundaries.

A Right to Fish Act is pending in Congress and in many state legislatures that would prevent officials from closing off fishing until and unless a specific cause of overfishing is identified and dealt with directly. All anglers are urged to support the right to fish principles in order to preserve non-commercial fishing on a sustainable basis.

Sources for reading about continuing developments regarding the no-fishing zones include the Coastal Conservation Association, American Sportfishing Association, Recreational Fishing Alliance and *Florida Sportsman* magazine.

It should be noted, however, that the controversies over marine reserves have nothing to do with limited prohibitions of fishing in certain spawning aggregation sites offshore.

Virtually all sportfishing conservationists support seasonal closures where spawning stocks have been overfished for market purposes.

The guiding principle must be to limit catches to no more than will renew themselves naturally, providing indefinite sustainability. SB

Sponge boat returns. Florida's live bottom sold in the gift shops.

trap about 90 percent of all material passing through them, according to researchers.

Why are sponges being harvested in some century-old tradition, with almost five million harvested annually in the Florida Keys alone? Mostly to satisfy the tourist industry; Florida sponges are hauled back to Fargo or Des Moines, among other places, often left on bookshelves as a memento of some family vacation long ago. Most are eventually thrown away. Some are sold as such vital commodities as additions to cosmetic kits, or for scrubbing cars. Synthetic substitutes are plentiful.

There has been no champion of the lowly sponge, no fund-raising dinners held, no lobbyists working in Washington or around the Gulf of Mexico Fishery Management Council, to prevent sponge boats from plying their trade.

Until legislation is introduced to stop sponging in Florida waters, all one can do is boycott those innocuous shops that sell natural Florida sponges. (Shell shops specialize in selling coral chunks, rare shells and other items pried from precious coral reefs around the world, but that is another matter that will have to be addressed in the future). SB

CHAPTER 17

Artificial Reefs

For centuries, artificial reefs so popular with fish were always accidental sinkings from ill-fated vessels in distress. There were many of those, but not enough to support today's fishing industry with many thousands of boats. So, fishermen began sinking their own debris offshore, adding to that number.

However, done without regulations or permits, the result was a mess of unstable materials that was neither suitable or acceptable. Today, after experience and research, stable underwater materials and designs are now being used. They provide habitat in many areas that very often are vast, sandy bottoms with no hard structure for corals to attach.

When it comes to reef-building policies, Florida bounced from one extreme to the other.

See DVD for more underwater wreck video.

Artificial reefs are proven habitat for coral growth and many species of reef fish. Countless fishermen depend on their availability.

Reefs Accidental and Intentional

The motto of many of the volunteers who build artificial reefs off coastal states in modern times has been, "If you build it, they will come."

They couldn't be more right. Creating habitat for a diverse community of marine life is satisfying work, especially for those who later view their project underwater, observing everything from big grouper and snapper to tiny ornamental fish and other marine life.

Reef-building anglers who stay in the boat are more interested in increasing their catch, of course. One fine example of a reef-building program is in Alabama, which has only one

Sunken vessels create an oasis in a sandy desert, attracting fish. This vessel is surrounded by underwater sand dunes sculpted by the currents.

percent of the Gulf's coastline, but whose anglers catch 40 percent of all red snapper landed each year. Their success is widely attributed to 2,500 square miles of Gulf bottom that the state permitted for artificial reefs, in 65 to 180 feet of water, which is prime turf for snapper and grouper. Thousands of reef sites have sprung up out there of all sizes. Add minimum sizes, closed seasons and bag limits, and their snapper fishing only gets better.

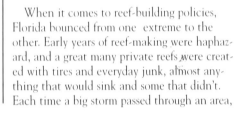

When it comes to reef-building policies, Florida bounced from one extreme to the other. Early years of reef-making were haphazard, and a great many private reefs were created with tires and everyday junk, almost anything that would sink and some that didn't. Each time a big storm passed through an area,

Reef materials are now chosen for their stability in the marine environment, to enhance existing bottom habitat, and to increase local fish populations. Many modern sites can now withstand a glancing blow from passing hurricanes.

underwater junk was scattered far and wide, usually lost to fishermen. Lots of tires wound up on the beach after a storm, among other items.

Florida's reef permitting system is now rigorous by comparison, with red tape, bottom areas inspected by divers for suitability, and reef materials cleaned and approved. Sites without a permit have actually been removed by the Coast Guard, especially in clear waters around the Keys on the Gulf side, where little hard structure exists. Fishermen who built those sites years ago were a little unhappy when their secret spots were abruptly pulled out and barged away to a landfill. Anglers today should keep in mind that it's now illegal to dump even a cinderblock offshore without a state permit. The Marine Patrol frowns on fishermen caught hauling material offshore for dumping.

Reef materials are now chosen for their stability in the marine environment, to enhance existing bottom habitat, and certainly to increase local fish populations. Many modern sites can withstand a brush from passing hurricanes. Derelict ships, concrete pipe and outdated bridge rubble are now materials of choice for bigger reefs. In addition, smaller sites are built of concrete modules, including igloos with holes cut in them, to allow passing fish traffic. The igloos are thick and very heavy, withstand storms, and their concrete has a pH chemistry that allows for maximum marine growth, such as coral. So even Florida's natural coral colonies, which have been degraded in recent years, have a chance to grow and reproduce, thanks to new, solid structure offshore—artificial reefs.

Because of the efforts of many nonprofit fishing and diving organizations in Florida, there are almost 1,900 artificial reefs in nearby state and federal waters. These include multiple but separate deployments on larger sites, with that total growing almost weekly. Even huge aircraft carriers are targets for the fish.

Florida also awards roughly $600,000 annually to help fund artificial reef programs. That money originates from state fishing licenses

Despite the name, "private reefs" aren't created for individual fishermen. The public can fish them.

These lucky anglers have just landed a pair of high-quality scamp grouper.

Concrete Reef Forms

One of the true success stories of improved reef design has been that of Reef Innovations, the Florida company that makes popular reef balls, which are concrete igloos weighing up to 1,500 pounds. They have numerous holes for fish to enter and leave, are virtually storm-proof, and they easily grow coral. Other coastal states have ordered these patented fish homes, or the molds to pour the concrete. (It seems that transporting heavy weight is costly, and it's better to mix and pour the concrete in a nearby seaport close to the drop site.)

Reef Balls are available in several sizes, some not so large. They've even been used around piers, private docks and seawalls to enhance habitat. Snapper and grouper living in bay waters would probably be quick to adopt one of these homes.

That has certainly been the case offshore where various concrete forms, including pyramids, have been sunk in waters up to 200 feet deep. SB

and federal funding for fish restoration. These reefs are so popular off tourism-oriented Palm Beach, Broward, Dade and Monroe counties, their value has been estimated to be worth several billion dollars.

Florida also issues about 20 grants each year to county governments, nonprofit organizations and universities that pursue reef-building initiatives or artificial-reef studies. About two thirds of those grants go to reefs in state waters and the remainder to projects in federal waters. Individual grants are used to place material,

Reef Balls made of heavy, durable concrete are installed to promote marine growth and to attract fish. These mangrove snappers appear ready to move in.

buy prefabricated modules, clean ships destined for sinking, and fund studies designed to improve the success of future artificial reefs. Scores of other new reefs and deployments are created without state support each year by other entities such as county governments, fishing clubs and reef-building organizations.

Florida and neighboring Alabama are the only states in the Gulf or Atlantic that still allow the construction of "private" reefs. Despite the name, these aren't reserved for particular fishermen. Rather, it means anyone can

Anglers having a good day while anchored or drifting over artificial reefs. Baitfish such as cigar minnows school above these reefs, readily available as live bait. Far below, snapper and grouper wait for something tasty to pass by.

are more complicated than merely dumping random material.

build a reef of suitable material, have it approved by the state, and then place it offshore where they want to within a permitted area. The big difference is that the location isn't published, which greatly adds to their value.

One group that has worked tirelessly (so to speak) is the Organization of Artificial Reefs (OAR), based out of Tallahassee. OAR volunteers have concentrated their huge efforts off Florida's Big Bend in the Gulf. There, they've built several dozen large reefs offshore that are host to many visiting boats each weekend

when the weather is agreeable. They even have their own divers do reliable bottom surveys before a site is chosen. They map out an area, testing for solid rock under the sand, while avoiding natural, live rock bottom, as well as mud. Surveys are important: Various artificial reefs in the Gulf have disappeared almost overnight because the site wasn't inspected and reef material, dumped over soft bottom, simply vanished underground.

At any rate, with their solid experience, there has been speculation the OAR group would make a good, state-wide organization with 401k status, which means donations would be eligible for a tax write-off. That seems like a quality investment in the future of offshore fishing, helping to build reefs that, coupled with experience gained refining them in the last 30 years, should keep them productive for a very long time.

Even the design of reefs has been improved upon a great deal. Effective artificial reefs with a diverse marine community are a little more complicated than merely dumping material overboard. Certain shapes and configurations work much better than others, for instance. And, by patiently doing fish counts on the bottom (often monitoring populations of resident gag grouper), divers have documented that small clusters of concrete cubes in a wider area were host to three times more grouper than a single, large mass of cubes, even when it contained more concrete than the others combined. SB

Applying for a Reef Grant

Fishermen interested in building a reef off-shore should know that the FWC's Artificial Reef Section sends out a request for grant proposals every year in January. Non-profit organizations who would like to receive such announcements from the state should call (850) 488-6058 for an application form.

Or, they can request an application through the FWC's Web site. More than a half million dollars are disbursed annually for such worthy goals.

To receive funding, recipient groups must already have the necessary state or federal permits in hand. Reef permits in state waters

LOCATING ARTIFICIAL REEFS

Artificial reef locations in Florida can be found at www.floridasportsman.com and at the Fish and Wildlife Conservation Commission's Web site at www.floridaconservation.org

Florida Sportsman Fishing Charts and others provide locations for many artificial reefs around the coast.

The combined efforts of government and community anglers led to the sinking of this 168-foot Army supply ship in January, 2003. Named for Florida Sportsman founder Karl Wickstrom, the vessel began attracting large amberjack, grouper and other species just days after it came to rest in 195 feet, some nine miles east of Stuart, Florida.

are provided by the Florida DEP through regional wetland resources offices and require the same formalities as filling out standard dredge and fill permits. Reef permits in federal waters farther offshore require dealing with the U.S. Army Corps of Engineers. SB

INDEX

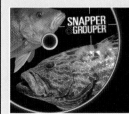

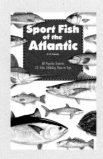
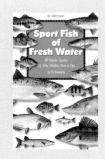

MAGS

Baits, Rigs & Tackle
Full color edition. Vic Dunaway's fishing bestseller covers exactly what is needed to get rigged.
$16.95

Florida Sportsman
Published monthly for Sunshine State anglers. Includes bonus coverage of the Caribbean.

NEW

Sportsman's Best Snapper & Grouper
First in series of informative how-to books. Includes DVD
$19.95

Shallow Water Angler
New from FS. Published quarterly for skinny–water fishermen from Maine to Texas.

FS Lawsticks
Now, also; Texas, Louisiana, Mississippi, Alabama, Georgia, North Carolina, South Carolina, Virginia and California.

Folding plastic **$4.95**
Clear Mylar **$3.95**

ALL-COLOR
Annual Fishing Planner
Florida tides & monthly tips. Know when and where to catch more fish. **$8.95**

Fishing Charts
24 regional Florida charts covering inshore and offshore. Includes GPS, boat ramps and fish ID.
$14.95 each

Wall Calendar
Fine art for your home or office. Each month has different art. Includes holidays, moon phases and seasons. **$9.95**